D1000244

SPECULUM ANNIVERSARY MONOGRAPHS
THREE

ENRIQUE IV AND THE CRISIS OF FIFTEENTH-CENTURY CASTILE

SPECULUM ANNIVERSARY MONOGRAPHS

THREE

ENRIQUE IV and the Crisis of Fifteenth-Century Castile 1425-1480

WILLIAM D. PHILLIPS, JR.

THE MEDIAEVAL ACADEMY OF AMERICA 1978

The publication of this book was made possible by funds contributed to the Mediaeval Academy during the Semi-Centennial Fund Drive.

LCC: 77-89931
ISBN: 910956-63-4
Printed in the United States of America

To my parents

Contents

Acknowledgments

While this book has been in preparation, first as a dissertation and later as it approached its final form, numerous scholars have willingly taken the time to discuss it, criticize it, and offer suggestions for its improvement. My gratitude to them is profound, and while I can never discharge the debts, I would like to acknowledge them. Marvin Lunenfeld was the first to offer me practical advice about research in Spain. Luis G. de Valdeavellano of the University of Madrid generously made the library of his seminar available to me. David Hicks of New York University chaired my dissertation committee, and Marshall Baldwin and Nicolás Sánchez-Albornoz were committee members. Thereafter, as I took the work through several drafts and many changes, I benefited from the perceptive readings done by John B. Owens, Peggy K. Liss, Erika Spivakovsky, Stanley Payne, and Daniel Eisenberg. It was Helen Nader who provided the perfect combination of criticism and enthusiasm for the manuscript that allowed me to recognize the overall shape it should have and to rectify many of its faults. The outside readers, who are unknown to me, offered many helpful suggestions. I wish to thank the Mediaeval Academy of America and the board of editors of "Speculum Anniversary Monographs," in particular Luke Wenger and Charles T. Davis, whose comments on the penultimate draft allowed me to improve the final one significantly.

I am grateful to the Graduate School of Arts and Science of New York University for a fellowship that allowed me to go to Spain for research for the dissertation. Since then, grants from the San Diego State University Foundation assisted me in some of my subsequent visits to Spain to do research.

Finally, my gratitude is deepest to my wife, Carla Rahn Phillips, for her support, encouragement, and love.

W. D. P.

I

ENRIQUE IV AND THE HISTORICAL RECORD

In Castile's transition from medieval to modern times, the fifteenth century was the crucial period that produced the institutions to sustain Spain's Golden Age. This proposition is familiar to students of Renaissance Europe, accustomed as they are to examining the origins of the new monarchies and the successful struggle of monarchs against their adversaries, from east to west across the continent. Equally well known is the assumption that in Spain Fernando and Isabel—the Catholic Monarchs—were the victors in the struggle and creators of the modern state. Not quite as familiar is the idea that continuity linked their policies with those of their Trastámara ancestors, who ruled in Castile from the mid-fourteenth century and in Aragon from the early fifteenth. Recent historians have come to see that Fernando and Isabel were reformers as well as innovators, building on the partially erected foundations of the past as they quelled the anarchy that the previous Castilian ruler Enrique IV had been unable to check. Yet almost no one has bothered to examine the received knowledge concerning Enrique systematically or to place his actions in their proper perspective.

Given the importance accorded to Fernando and Isabel, it is almost shocking to assert that in many respects Isabel had a worthy predecessor in her half brother Enrique, Castile's most maligned ruler. His twenty-year reign (from 1454 to 1474) is crucial in the development of the Castilian monarchy. The chaos of the last years of his reign is amply documented, but few historians have recognized that, despite the failures, Enrique introduced numerous policies that would be perfected in the reign of his successor. A fresh interpretation of the last years of Castile's separate existence and the role of Enrique IV in those years is long overdue.

But before a more accurate appraisal of Enrique IV can be offered, the accumulated historical record must be examined and faulty or mistaken assumptions identified and rejected. In the five centuries since his death chroniclers and historians have subjected him to an almost constant stream of scorn and abuse. According to conventional wisdom he was personally inept, politically incompetent, and physiologically impotent. Supposedly, Enrique had no plans for his kingdom and allowed a series of corrupt royal favorites to dictate his every move. He was even considered incapable of producing an heir; so Juana, the daughter born to his wife, must not have been his, but a child of one of his followers—Beltrán de la Cueva. This impression dictated the names history has bestowed on them: Enrique *el Impotente* and Juana *la Beltraneja*. Because of a lack of direction, the story goes, Castile slipped into economic collapse, political anarchy, civil war, and religious impiety. It fell to Isabel, the destined ruler, to reverse the slide and set Castile on the path to greatness. Since Isabel occupies such an exalted, quasi-religious position in Spanish history, most historians have chosen to treat her reign either as a spontaneous generation which owed nothing to the past or as a return to the supposed Christian purity of the Visigothic monarchy after seven centuries of Muslim domination and Jewish influence. In both cases, such historians agree that the reign of Enrique IV was the nadir of the Castilian monarchy and go to great lengths to exaggerate his shortcomings in order to make Isabel seem all the more glorious.

Such ideas were first put forth in the fifteenth and sixteenth centuries by chroniclers who favored Isabel *la Católica*. The chronicles of the period echoed the profound divisions the war of succession engendered. Due to the divergent political affiliations of fifteenth-century Castile, Enrique's reign brought forth more than one firsthand interpretation, but the prevailing modern view largely relies on the foundation of misinformation provided by Alonso de Palencia.[1] Of *converso* origin, Palencia was born in Osma in June of 1423. After spending time in Italy, Palencia became chronicler of Castile in 1456. When a group of nobles raised Enrique's half brother Alfonso to the role of rival king with a ceremony in Avila, Palencia was in the rebel band and thereafter acted as the ambassador of the archbishop of Toledo to present the views of Alfonso's faction to the Holy See. On the death of Alfonso, Palencia gave his support to Isabel and served as her ambassador to the court of Juan II of Aragon, where he laid the foun-

1. For a discussion of this see: Juan Torres Fontes, *Estudio sobre la "Crónica de Enrique IV" del Dr. Galíndez de Carvajal* (Murcia, 1946); Julio Puyol Alonso, "Los cronistas de Enrique IV," *Boletín de la Real Academia de la Historia* 78–79 (1921), passim; and the Introduction to *Biblioteca de autores españoles*, 70 (Madrid, 1953).

dation for the marriage negotiations between Fernando and the Castilian princess.

With such a political commitment, it is not surprising that when Palencia produced his chronicle—the *Décadas*—he presented his subject in a most unflattering light. He was extremely hostile to Enrique and portrayed the king and his followers as sexually perverted and religiously lax, if not actually heretical. For Palencia, Enrique's reign was an unrelieved disaster. By emphasizing the evil conditions the war of succession produced, and by magnifying the hardships Isabel faced, Palencia made her renewal of the kingdom seem more brilliant than it was.[2] Modern scholars have differing views regarding Palencia. Antonio Paz y Meliá extolled the virtues of Palencia as politician and historian, but the more accurate judgment is that of Julio Puyol: "men so passionate as [Palencia], and who take a direct part in the politics of their epoch, can make history, but not write it."[3]

Diego Enríquez del Castillo presented Enrique's side in the struggle. A native of Segovia, Enríquez del Castillo was born in 1443 and entered royal service when Enrique IV became king, holding offices as chaplain, counsellor, and chronicler. Although he clearly favored Enrique, Enríquez was not a blind partisan and occasionally he censured the king's actions. He saw Enrique as beneficent, but weak, and ascribed his failures to the deceptions of his trusted nobles. The *Crónica de Enrique IV*, begun during the king's lifetime and completed shortly after his death, suffers from the loss of the first draft when Enríquez was imprisoned in Segovia by the rebellious faction. Since he had to reproduce it from memory, the earlier part of his chronicle cannot be accepted with the same assurance as the later portions.[4] Puyol believed that the passages which are unfavorable to Enrique may be the product of a later stage in the chronicler's life. After the accession of Isabel, Enríquez may have tried to obtain a position in her court and perhaps when he rewrote the lost portion of his chronicle he included material critical of Enrique in order to win the queen's favor.[5]

One contemporary writer who provided unswerving praise for Enrique IV was Rodrigo (or Ruy) Sánchez de Arévalo (1404-1470), a cleric and recipient of a doctorate from Salamanca. While holding a series of ecclesi-

2. Torres Fontes, *Estudio*, pp. 11–12, 28–29. See also Antonio Paz y Meliá, *El cronista Alonso de Palencia: Su vida y sus obras, sus Décadas y las crónicas contemporáneas* (Madrid, 1914).

3. Paz y Meliá, *Alonso de Palencia*, p. xxxviii; Puyol, "Los cronistas," 79:28.

4. Torres Fontes, *Estudio*, pp. 11–12, 29–30.

5. Puyol, "Los cronistas," 78:412–14.

astical positions, Sánchez served both Juan II and Enrique IV as an ambassador to the papacy. He produced a number of Latin writings, among them the *Compendiosa Historia Hispanica*, written at the request of Enrique IV and first printed in Rome in 1470. In his history he depicted the king as a strong monarch, the paradigm of all kingly virtues. Such an unclouded vision of Enrique, so alien from other contemporary writers, warrants attention as the favorable judgment of a qualified, intelligent observer, but it cannot command unquestioning acceptance. Sánchez was a loyal traditionalist and a staunch partisan of monarchy and papacy, so he may have demonstrated undue respect for Enrique simply because he was Castile's monarch. Sánchez was generally absent from Castile from the late 1450s until his death, and as a result was not a firsthand witness of the events there. We also should consider the brief work he produced during 1456 and 1457, *El vergel de los príncipes*, one of his two Castilian works. This mirror for a prince, dedicated to Enrique IV, is a treatise on suitable amusements for nobles, and, as Trame has suggested, it may have been a subtle admonition to persuade the king that moderation was the best course.[6]

Diego de Valera was born in Cuenca in 1402 or 1412, visited Bohemia, and in the reign of Isabel held many important royal posts. He was a poet and genealogist and the author of works of moral philosophy. Influenced by humanism, he modelled his writings on Sallust and Tacitus. As a historian he produced the *Memorial de diversas hazañas*, probably written in the 1480s, which drew to some extent on the work of Palencia but more heavily on the anonymous *Crónica castellana*. His personal acquaintance with the events and his lack of passion make his account seem reliable; Puyol felt the *Memorial* may be the best chronicle of Enrique's reign. Valera refused to place as much weight as Palencia on Enrique's imperfections and suggested that most of the monarch's problems were a result of the rebellious nobles.[7]

The final chronicler with a firsthand knowledge of the events of the pre-Isabelline monarchy was Fernando del Pulgar, born near Toledo in

6. Ibid., p. 488; Robert B. Tate, *Ensayos sobre la historiografía peninsular del siglo XV*, trans. Jesus Días (Madrid, 1970), pp. 74–104. His biography is provided by Richard H. Trame, *Rodrigo Sánchez de Arévalo, 1404-1470: Spanish Diplomat and Champion of the Papacy* (Washington, D.C., 1958). The portion of the *Historia Hispanica* covering the reign of Enrique IV was printed in a Madrid edition of 1787. *El vergel de los príncipes*, ed. Mario Penna, can be found in *Biblioteca de autores españoles*, 116 (Madrid, 1959).

7. Torres Fontes, *Estudio*, pp. 11–12, 31–32; Puyol, "Los cronistas," 79:119–26; Adolfo Bonilla y San Martín, *Fernando de Córdoba (1425-1486) y los orígenes del renacimiento filosófico en España* (Madrid, 1911), p. 27.

1436 and educated in the courts of Juan II and Enrique IV. He later acted as an ambassador of the *Reyes Católicos*, and in 1482 they commissioned him to write a chronicle of their reign. He produced a history which took the story of their rule up to about 1492. The first twenty chapters were concerned with Enrique. According to Puyol, the *Reyes Católicos* instructed Pulgar to produce a justification of Isabel's assumption of the crown and to use calumny against Enrique to support the rectitude of her action. Pulgar also wrote *Claros varones de Castilla*, a series of short biographies of the most influential figures in Castilian history in the later fifteenth century. His point of view was clearly biased against Enrique, but *Claros varones* was more balanced than his other works.[8]

In the early sixteenth century, Lorenzo Galíndez de Carvajal undertook a synthesis of these opposing viewpoints. Galíndez was a lawyer trained at the University of Salamanca. While working in the chancellery at Valladolid, he was appointed to the royal council of Fernando and Isabel. He assisted in the drafting of Isabel's will and served as Fernando's advisor after the queen's death. He also aided Carlos I in gaining title to the throne. Galíndez's *Crónica de Enrique IV* was a compendium and co-ordination of the positions expressed by the contemporary chroniclers. Although doubtlessly favorable to Isabel, he did not go to the same extremes as Palencia. His work is valuable because he was close enough to the events to possess virtually all the facts, and far enough away from them to avoid passionate partisanship.[9]

While the period is well served by the chronicles, their coverage is limited and other documentation is incomplete, scattered, and fugitive; time has dealt harshly with it. Fires in the *alcázar* of Madrid and the chancellery of Valladolid destroyed many important sources. Of the remaining documents, virtually all are official, and we have almost no personal letters from the king or his retinue and few direct quotations except for those the chroniclers recorded. As important, there is abundant evidence that Isabel conducted an intense campaign of historical revision—having chronicles rewritten and documents altered to suit and justify her position.[10] Consequently, an incomplete documentary record has led generations of historians to questionable assertions, forcing the modern investigator to

8. Torres Fontes, *Estudio*, pp. 11–12, 32–33; Puyol, "Los cronistas," 79:131–32, 143.

9. Torres Fontes, *Estudio*, pp. 9–23. Galíndez's *Crónica* is printed on pages 67–460.

10. For Isabel's chronicle revisions see Puyol, "Los cronistas," passim. For examples of the recasting of documents see Jaime Vicens Vives, *Historia crítica de la vida y reinado de Fernando II de Aragón* (Zaragoza, 1962), pp. 210, 237–42, 283–87.

use extraordinary care in assembling and weighing the available evidence. Because earlier historians relied heavily on the chronicles, they naturally repeated the concerns of the contemporary authors: court life, the personalities of the elite, and only the most significant political decisions. More can be done with archival records. They offer a broader perspective, allowing a view of the economy and the society and illuminating the underpinnings of political events, but systematic archival work on the subject has been begun only in recent times.

Most interpretations during the last hundred years have followed the views of the respected American historian William H. Prescott. Writing in the 1830s, Prescott's romantic temperament led him to portray Enrique as a wicked despot, his despotism tempered only by incompetence, and Isabel as the personification of clear-sighted progressivism and benign constitutionalism. Prescott allowed himself to use vicious *ad hominem* attacks on Enrique. He obscured the king's political dealings with censorious comments on his private and personal affairs. In relating the story of Enrique's supposed impotence, Prescott said that Enrique was "addicted from his earliest youth to debauchery, and when he had lost the powers, he retained all the relish, for the brutish pleasures of a voluptuary."[11] Prescott accused Enrique of embezzling money raised by papal crusading bulls to enrich his followers and himself, allowing anarchy to rage in Castile, and refusing to ensure the administration of justice.

Prescott's magnificent, flowing, opinionated prose makes it impossible not to quote him extensively. Here he contrasted the young Isabel with her brother:

> Her sedate conduct, and the decorum maintained in her court, formed a strong contrast with the frivolity and license which disgraced that of Henry and his consort. Thinking men were led to conclude that the sagacious administration of Isabella must eventually secure to her the ascendency over her rival; while all, who sincerely loved their country, could not but prognosticate for it, under her beneficent sway, a degree of prosperity, which it could never reach under the rapacious and profligate ministers who directed the councils of Henry, and most probably would continue to direct those of his daughter.[12]

Enrique's daughter Juana was born in 1462 and rumors arose naming Beltrán de la Cueva, the king's favorite, as her father. The question of

11. William H. Prescott, *History of the Reign of Ferdinand and Isabella the Catholic*, 3 vols. (Philadelphia, 1872), 1:164.
12. Ibid., 1:222–23.

Juana's legitimacy has been argued at length by modern historians, just as it was argued by her contemporaries. If she indeed was the king's legal child then Isabel's assumption of the throne was clearly illegal. Prescott, even though he was an ardent champion of Isabel, left the question in doubt. Most nobles acknowledged Juana as the king's heir shortly after her birth but, Prescott said, they may have been forced to do so. Enrique did agree to recognize Isabel as his heir at Toros de Guisando in 1468, but he withdrew his recognition when she married Fernando without his sanction. Prescott believed that Enrique left no will when he died in 1474, but Prescott was forced to admit the possibility of an oral testament in favor of his daughter. Nevertheless, Prescott still regarded Isabel as ideally, if not legally, the proper successor to the king who through his "drivelling imbecility" had brought the "fortunes of the kingdom . . . to the lowest ebb since the great Saracen invasion."[13]

Prescott belabored the sensational at the expense of the mundane and practical. In a telling passage Prescott revealed the tremendous chasm between himself and modern historians. He reported Enrique's "unconstitutional and oppressive acts," including "attempts at arbitrary taxation, interference in the freedom of elections, and in the right exercised by the cities in nominating the commanders of such contingents of troops as they might contribute to the public defense." Also, the "territories of towns were repeatedly alienated."[14] The modern historian would point out that, legal and honorable or not, these were useful and necessary measures often used by the monarchs of the fifteenth and sixteenth centuries for increasing their power.

Toward the end of the nineteenth century, J. H. Mariéjol published his *L'Espagne sous Ferdinand et Isabelle*. In the short space devoted to Enrique and his reign, Mariéjol arrived at a somewhat altered view of the king. Like Prescott, he declined to accept Juana's legitimacy, basing his position on the widespread disbelief among the nobility that she was the king's child. Mariéjol saw Enrique's acceptance of Isabel at Toros de Guisando as the only means at his disposal to check the growing revolt. Thereafter he made every effort to secure an incompetent husband for Isabel, one who would prove such a disadvantage that Juana, "whom he insisted on regarding as his own flesh and blood," would triumph.[15] By this approach Mariéjol did

13. Ibid., 1:233–34.

14. Ibid., 1:166–67.

15. J.H. Mariéjol, *The Spain of Ferdinand and Isabella*, trans. Benjamin Keen (New Brunswick, N.J., 1961), p. 9, originally published under the title *L'Espagne sous*

credit Enrique with a conscious policy, unlike the aimless inconsistency reported by Prescott. He remained, nonetheless, censorious of "this prince who left to his successors not only a heritage of a half-century of factional struggles, [and] of feudal anarchy, but [also] a war of succession."[16]

In 1918 R. B. Merriman published the first two volumes of his massive work, *The Rise of the Spanish Empire in the Old World and the New.* As his title indicates, his emphasis was primarily on the imperial ventures of Spain, but in passing he provided an important synthesis of the internal history of the Iberian peninsula, based on a wide-ranging study of printed documents. His discussion of Enrique IV was short and relied to a large extent upon the interpretations of Prescott and Mariéjol. For instance, he repeated Prescott on the supposedly evil moral tenor of life at the court, but Merriman did not denigrate Enrique to the extent Prescott had. Rather he saw him as a weak king, dominated by a "natural indolence," who was willing to let events evolve instead of trying to control them, and who procrastinated and delegated authority. Merriman felt that the irregularities of Enrique's personal life made it difficult for him to arrest the opposition to his political actions.

Merriman's contribution was his emphasis on the considerations of diplomacy which affected Enrique and his subjects. The earlier historians had written from almost a purely Castilian viewpoint; Merriman showed the important influence of Aragon, France, and Portugal on Castilian affairs. For example, in 1462 Enrique had encouraged the Catalan revolt against Juan II of Aragon with troops and money. Louis XI of France acted as mediator the next year, and Enrique agreed to abandon the Catalan rebels in return for some minor concessions from Juan. Merriman said that this infuriated many of the Castilian noblemen who sought gains for themselves in the lands of the Aragonese king.

Merriman also showed that foreign considerations helped to bring many nobles to Isabel's side when Enrique renounced the pact of Toros de Guisando after Isabel married Fernando without his permission. The tide of popularity flowing toward Isabel was strengthened when Enrique secured the engagement of Juana with the duke of Guienne, brother of Louis of France. In a spirit of nascent nationalism, Merriman believed, the Castilian lords rejected the prospect of French influence. Even after the duke of

Ferdinand et Isabelle (Paris, 1892). Keen's introduction to the English edition provides a fine survey of later historiography to 1961.

16. Ibid., p. 15.

Guienne renounced the match, this spirit continued, adversely affecting Enrique's delicate negotiations with France. Merriman did consider Juana as unquestionably the legal heir of Enrique; for Merriman there was assuredly a deathbed will. Her legitimacy and right of succession were above reproach:

> She was . . . the daughter of the queen of Castile, born in the royal palace, and the allegations of her foes in regard to her paternity were never definitely proved. Finally, she had been formally acknowledged and sworn to by the Castilian Cortes as the heiress of the realm, and had been recognized as such by King Henry.[17]

In spite of this, Isabel personified the real interests of Castile for Merriman. The many nobles who rallied to her side saw her as the ultimate victor and wished to be on the winning side.

J. B. Sitges produced a volume in 1912 entitled *Enrique IV y la excelente Señora . . . Doña Juana La Beltraneja*. Sitges intended to rehabilitate Juana and to absolve her from the imputation of illegitimacy. In so doing, he provided an improved view of Enrique, a monarch who was weak and vacillating, though kind and well intentioned. Sitges produced evidence from contemporaries reporting Enrique to be fully capable of producing an heir. He also used Portuguese sources to show that Juana was regarded as legitimate in Portugal.[18]

A work of great interest but limited usefulness is J. Lucas-Dubreton's *El rey huraño: Enrique IV de Castilla y su época*. The emphasis here was on the epoch. A twentieth-century romantic, Lucas-Dubreton concerned himself with painting a brilliant canvas that emphasized intrigue and picturesque details. It is not really a scholarly study of the Castilian monarchy, but at his best Lucas-Dubreton offers some interesting sidelights.[19]

A medical analysis of the king done in the 1930s by Gregorio Marañón, a physician and historian, provides a fascinating interpretation of the debate over Juana. *Post facto* medical reconstructions are suspect in cases of such slim evidence, but Marañón was not deterred. His view was that Enrique was a homosexual. In an attempt to divert attention from this fact, the

17. R.B. Merriman, *The Rise of the Spanish Empire in the Old World and the New*, 2: *The Catholic Kings* (New York, 1918), p. 49.
18. J.B. Sitges, *Enrique IV y la excelente Señora llamada vulgarmente Doña Juana La Beltraneja, 1425-1530* (Madrid, 1912), passim.
19. J. Lucas-Dubreton, *El rey huraño: Enrique IV de Castilla y su época*, trans. J. García Mercadal (Madrid, 1945), passim. The book was first published in French (Paris, 1922).

king married twice, paraded a series of mistresses before the court, and may even have encouraged his wife's relations with Beltrán de la Cueva. Nevertheless, after considering the weight of evidence concerning his impotence, Marañón concluded that Enrique may well have been only partially impotent and still capable of producing an heir.[20]

The first important modern revisionist is Orestes Ferrara, who presented Enrique in quite a different light in *Un pleito sucesorio*, published in 1945. His main point is the assertion that Juana was indeed the king's legitimate daughter and legal heir. The victory of the *Reyes Católicos*, then, was purely a usurpation. "The triumph of the collateral branch over the direct branch was dictated by arms and not by law."[21] The revolt of the nobles who raised first Alfonso and then Isabel as rival claimants to Enrique's throne showed no initial concern over Juana or her paternity. It was from the first a revolt against the king.

The reasons Ferrara gave for the genesis of the revolt provide a drastic rehabilitation of the much assailed ruler. The nobles were reacting against Enrique's attempts at consolidating the apparatus of government. Anarchy erupted because Enrique was becoming too strong, rather than because of his political incompetence. The revolt finally succeeded due to Enrique's reluctance to follow up his advantages. He desired peace, not because of personal fear or laziness, but because he hated the devastation that would result from war. He was driven into war only after all options failed.

Un pleito sucesorio is almost completely a dialogue with and refutation of the fifteenth-century chroniclers, whose veracity and honesty Ferrara questioned, especially in the case of Palencia. Either they wrote propaganda for Isabel, or she had their works altered to suit her needs. His approach is intriguing but difficult to execute successfully. Ferrara's book does not have a foundation in archival work. He wrote his study from the old chronicles, often citing them only to refute their interpretations, and the main support for his own contentions was the negative evidence from the chronicles. Even the work of Enríquez del Castillo, the one major chronicler favorable to the king, does not fully support Ferrara's claims.

20. Gregorio Marañón, *Ensayo biológico sobre Enrique IV de Castilla y su tiempo*, 10th ed. (Madrid, 1964); first published as "Ensayo biológico sobre Enrique IV de Castilla," *Boletín de la Real Academia de la Historia* 96 (1930):11–93. See the recent critique by Daniel Eisenberg, "Enrique IV and Gregorio Marañón," *Renaissance Quarterly* 27 (1976):21–29.

21. Orestes Ferrara, *Un pleito sucesorio: Enrique IV, Isabel de Castilla y La Beltraneja* (Madrid, 1945), p. 340.

His desire to redress the balance made him incautious, and he allowed the pendulum to swing too far toward Enrique's side.

Antonio Bermejo de la Rica produced a useful critical summary of the reign of Enrique IV in 1945. No revisionist, Bermejo wrote in the old tradition, censuring Enrique and asserting his supposed incompetence. Bermejo disliked Enrique's new appointees and castigated his lack of a vigorous prosecution of the Granadan war. The civil war, for Bermejo, represented justifiably outraged feelings on the part of the nobles and brought forth anarchy, weakened morality, and disrespect for hierarchy and discipline.[22] He regarded Enrique as a sad figure caught and destroyed by "the irredeemable weakness of a man who, born to occupy a glorious throne, sank into all the most somber abysses of disgrace."[23]

The great Catalan historian Jaime Vicens Vives never produced a study devoted to Enrique, but in several of his works he generally supported the revisionist viewpoint best expressed by Ferrara. Vicens believed that Enrique had a "truly revolutionary" program for the restructuring of the royal government but lacked the ability to carry it out.[24] He was not an entirely incapable monarch and showed particular skill in using his position to advantage during the Catalan revolt.[25] According to Vicens, Juana was unquestionably the daughter of Enrique IV, whose policies "had nothing to do with true or imagined personal weakness."[26]

A recent synthesis and re-examination of the whole period was done by Luis Suárez Fernández in a section (1964) of the massive *Historia de España* edited by Ramón Menéndez Pidal. In a masterful review of the previous studies the author introduced a considerable amount of new primary materials and devoted more attention to the economy and society. According to Suárez Fernández, Enrique was a good and able ruler in the early years of his reign. His downward path commenced when he lost the support and good will of some of the nobles. First he aroused their apprehensions by showing lack of confidence in the nobles as the traditional advisers of the king, systematically raising men of lower rank, simple *hidalgos*, into positions of prestige and power. The most notable example, Beltrán de la

22. Antonio Bermejo de la Rica, *El triste destino de Enrique IV y La Beltraneja* (Madrid, n. d. [1945]), pp. 143, 149–50, 175, 200.
23. Ibid., p. 241.
24. Jaime Vicens Vives, *Approaches to the History of Spain*, trans. Joan C. Ullman (Berkeley and Los Angeles, 1967), pp. 82–83.
25. Vicens, *Fernando II*, p. 216.
26. Jaime Vicens Vives, *Juan II de Aragón (1398-1479): Monarquía y revolución en la España del siglo XV* (Barcelona, 1953), p. 28.

Cueva, was also among the most unpopular. Enrique lost further support by refusing to press the war with Granada, preferring to deal diplomatically with the Muslims. Suárez Fernández was sure that while Juana was legally Enrique's daughter, the agreement of Toros de Guisando gave Isabel an indisputable right to the crown.[27]

According to Suárez the anarchy which ensued after the marriage of Fernando and Isabel was exacerbated by economic depression. "By the skill or stupidity of Enrique IV, the coinage had been adulterated, and as an extreme remedy the situation had proceeded to the suspension of minting and an accelerated devaluation of that [coinage] still in circulation."[28]

Suárez Fernández rightly credited Enrique with creating an instrument against unrest which proved invaluable for Isabel when she gained the throne. This was the reorganized *Hermandad*, the local peace-keeping force of the Castilian towns. Although Suárez missed the early moves, he did report that Enrique IV worked out the organizational agreement with civic representatives at Villacastín the year before his death, too late to use the *Hermandad* to reassert control over the kingdom.[29]

Enrique and the other main characters—Isabel, Fernando, and Juana—are curiously indistinct in Suárez's account. Far more important for him were the great noble families, the *clanes familiares*, in whose actions Suárez found the key for his interpretation of the period. The clans sought to extend their own power and struggled among themselves as well as with the monarch. The great nobles raised Isabel's prospects and doomed to failure any policies attempted by Enrique. The adherence of a large group of noble families assured Isabel's ultimate victory.

With a firm command of the traditional sources and modern studies, supplemented by some archival work, Suárez is often correct in the specifics, but his general interpretations are open to question. In his enormously influential *Nobleza y monarquía*, published in 1959 and issued in a revised edition in 1975, he depicts Castile's fifteenth century as the stage of a revolutionary confrontation between the nobility and the monarchy. He holds that many nobles wished to dilute the authority of the crown

27. See the special studies of this topic by Suárez: "En torno al pacto de los Toros de Guisando," *Hispania* 23 (1963):344–65; and with Vicente Rodríguez Valencia, *Matrimonio y derecho sucesorio de Isabel la Católica* (Valladolid, 1960), p. 123.

28. Luis Suárez Fernández, "Los Trastámaras de Castilla y Aragón en el siglo XV (1407-74)," in vol. 15 of *Historia de España*, ed. Ramón Menéndez Pidal (Madrid, 1964), p. 301. See also, Suárez Fernández's *Nobelza y monarquía: Puntos de vista sobre la historia castellana del siglo XV* (Valladolid, 1959; 2nd. ed., 1975).

29. Suárez, "*Los Trastámaras*," pp. 271–272, 310.

and reduce the monarch to a *primus inter pares*. "The nobility, for its part, aspired to give the *res publica* a more decidedly contractual structure, closing the monarchy in a fairly tight circle of rights and duties in relation to those very few lines who joined wealth and power."[30] His arguments are eloquent, but perhaps not thoroughly consistent. At times he speaks of the nobility as an oligarchy that had closed ranks against the crown; at others he seeks to identify royalists—in particular the Mendoza family—and anti-royalists. It is possible to propose a more satisfying counterargument, one that eliminates the need to distinguish ideological parties—where none really existed—and places the conflict at a more fundamental and realistic level. There was no "revolutionary" confrontation; the nobles never proposed anything like an alternative to the existence of the hereditary monarchy. The closest they came was the Sentence of Medina del Campo, yet this document would have served only to institutionalize their advisory role by giving them a veto over certain royal decisions, and it was supported by no more than a fraction of the nobles. Enrique's noble backers followed him into battle rather than have him accept the Sentence.

If there was no revolution, can we identify consistent royalists and anti-royalists? Perhaps in a few cases. There were nobles who worked to weaken the monarchy's freedom of action, and there were others who tried to strengthen it. Yet membership in the opposing camps was always fluid and non-ideological; even the Mendozas were motivated occasionally by pure self-interest. In contrast to Suárez's assertion, the *grandes* of Castile never consituted a noble oligarchy, and they were always flexible enough to support whoever could be relied upon to give them the greatest benefits. They were almost exclusively swayed by the desire to expand or secure their possessions and positions. Their allegiances varied with time and situation, depending on whether they saw the monarch or his antagonists as their best hope. In suggesting an ideological interpretation, Suárez strives too vigorously to impose order on a fluid situation.

In 1964 Tarsicio de Azcona published *Isabel la Católica*, the best and most measured biography of the queen to date, based on wide-ranging archival investigations. In the course of the book he suggests a number of improved viewpoints regarding Enrique. He affirms and documents that the first ten years of Enrique's reign were successful, an old idea in need of restating. Enrique and Isabel always dealt with one another with fraternal good will. Juana could doubtlessly have been the king's daughter. Enrique foreshadowed Isabel in his attempt to establish an inquisition. Yet, while

30. Suárez, *Nobleza y monarquía*, pp. 10–11.

he provides new ideas merely by taking an objective look at the documents, Azcona finds it necessary to offer a kind of apology.

> We are fully convinced that Isabel of Castile has nothing to fear from history, from a documented history, removed from the frenzy of human passions, and, therefore, [she] has nothing to fear from a more just evaluation of her half brother Enrique IV and her cousin Juana of Castile.[31]

A recent biography of Enrique IV and the first in English is that of Townsend Miller, who ignores the newer interpretations of specialists and repeats the traditional, unrevised account, enlivening it with extensive discussion of the sexual irregularities of the dramatis personae. It is a limited work, since Miller deals nearly exclusively with the political history, scandals, and imbroglios of the court and the high nobility, while neglecting the lower orders of society almost totally. He dismisses the Basques, who were among the most successful sea traders of Europe, as "that savage race." Two of the most significant developments in fifteenth-century Castile were the increasing economic control by the nobility and the movements and attitudes leading to the Inquisition. On the first point Miller is totally silent; far from examining noble opposition to Enrique in economic terms, he does not even discuss the Mesta. He is even more misguided in his treatment of the relations among the various religions of the peninsula. Contrary to all objective scholarship, he implies long-standing, inexorable Christian-Muslim hostility, which in reality was not yet fully developed. In a field where there are more questions than firm answers and where the existing documents are often contradictory, Miller is too confident of his conclusions. Ample evidence for at least a partial rehabilitation of Enrique's kingship exists, but Miller, in spite of his professed fondness for the monarch, has not bothered to uncover it. He neglects the archives and bases his narrative on the most hostile of the contemporary chroniclers. Because of its narrow focus and its failure to incorporate the findings of recent scholarship, his book is superficial and fails to advance the quest for an objective view of Enrique IV.[32]

31. Tarsicio de Azcona, *Isabel la Católica: Estudio crítico de su vida y su reinado* (Madrid, 1964), p. 45.
32. Townsend Miller, *Henry IV of Castile, 1425-1474* (Philadelphia and New York, 1972), passim. A more recent biography is that of Elías Amézaga, *Enrique Cuarto* (Madrid, 1974). The book offers little. It is not footnoted, and Amézaga invents dialogue for his characters and puts thoughts in their minds.

A synthesis of these conflicting viewpoints would provide answers to some questions of Enrique's reign, yet many questions would remain unanswered. Also, these interpretations themselves suggest still other problems. The whole succession crisis has never been treated satisfactorily, in particular Enrique's acquiescence in the face of Isabel's demands at Toros de Guisando. Also, why could Enrique not gain the support of a larger part of the nobility? If some nobles feared the influence of Portugal and France, there were others who feared Aragonese power. Why was Enrique unable to rally this group after Isabel's marriage? The measures Enrique introduced, if they had been successful, might have made him as powerful a ruler as Isabel later became. His attempts to increase taxation, control elections, reorganize the *Hermandad*, and obtain lasting diplomatic alliances were all far-sighted means by which he could have created a secure monarchy. Was his political incompetence so all-encompassing that it caused all of these efforts to be wasted? Were there other reasons for his failure? Enrique's predecessors had conducted diplomatic negotiations with the Muslim state of Granada in a tradition of accommodation and mutual tolerance. Yet Enrique aroused fierce opposition when he followed tradition in his dealings with the Muslims. Why did such an attitude develop at this time?

Hostility toward Jews and *conversos* was growing throughout Enrique's reign. Why did his policies toward non-Christians and new Christians fail? Why did he decline to institute a full-fledged inquisition to investigate *conversos*? Isabel was willing to do so and to use its special courts as an extension of royal administration. Was Enrique genuinely tolerant or merely shortsighted politically?

With these points unresolved a clear delineation of the king and his reign is impossible. Some questions, of course, can never be answered. The sources for a psychological portrait of the king simply do not exist, to take only one possible approach to a reinterpretation of Enrique. However, by careful examination of the chronicles dealing with him (which all too often have been excerpted to support particular interpretations) and by the introduction of other documentary material, both printed and archival, a much more favorable impression of the king develops. He was, of course, an unsuccessful king, and his reign can never be termed a brilliant one. But despite his ultimate failure, he must be seen as something more than a mindless creature governed by the fates and the clever manipulations of his courtiers. He had solid, well-conceived programs to bolster his own authority and improve the economy and administration of his kingdom, but

II

THE STAGE AND THE PLAYERS

The kingdom Enrique IV was to rule covered a wide swath of the central portion of the peninsula from the Bay of Biscay to the Mediterranean and the Atlantic. The title he was to bear indicated the long process of nation building in the intermittent reconquest: King of Castile, León, Toledo, Galicia, Murcia, Jaén, Córdoba, and Seville; Lord of Molina and Vizcaya. Enrique IV was able to add Gibraltar to this list.

Then as now regionalism was important. The rugged topography of the Iberian peninsula divided Castile into four different economic and geographic zones.[1] The first, in the extreme north, encompassed the coast of the Bay of Biscay and the northern slopes of the Cantabrian and Asturian mountains from the Pyrenees to the Atlantic, from the Basque provinces to Galicia. Small farming by peasant proprietors was the rule in this region, an area which the Muslims had never dominated. In the humid, green valleys and hillsides the characteristic economic activities included farming for local markets, viticulture (more extensive then than now), and dairy farming. Although unfavorable climatic conditions forced the inhabitants of the Cantabrian coast to import a large part of their grain from Old Castile and Andalusia, they found compensation in the wealth of forest products—timber, edible nuts, and fruits, especially the apple, which was used

1. For general accounts of the economy of Castile, see Luis Suárez Fernández, "Los Trastámaras de Castilla y Aragón en el siglo XV (1407-74)," in vol. 15 of *Historia de España*, ed. Ramón Menéndez Pidal (Madrid, 1964), pp. 5–11, and Jaime Vicens Vives, with Jorge Nadal, *An Economic History of Spain*, trans. Frances M. López-Morillas (Princeton, 1969), pp. 241–88. These two selections have been translated and reprinted in Roger Highfield, ed., *Spain in the Fifteenth Century* (New York and London, 1972), pp. 36–57, 81–112. For viticulture see Alain Huetz de Lemps, *Vignobles et vins du nord-ouest de l'Espagne*, 2 vols. (Bordeaux, 1967), 1:165-217. For dairy herding see Charles Julian Bishko, "The Peninsular Background of Latin American Cattle Ranching," *Hispanic American Historical Review* 32 (1952):493–94. For the best social and economic treatment of a northern area, see José Angel García de Cortázar, *Vizcaya en el siglo XV: Aspectos sociales y económicos* (Bilbao, 1966).

for cider—and fresh and saltwater fish. The iron of the eastern sector and the wool produced elsewhere in the kingdom were exported from the prosperous Cantabrian ports—Bilbao, Laredo, Castro Urdiales, San Vicente de la Barquera, San Sebastián, and Santander, among others, which were the heart of the Atlantic shipping trade, an aspect of the region's economic life that will be discussed later. For centuries European pilgrims had journeyed to the Galician shrine of Santiago de Compostela. While most of the pilgrims came on foot along the *camino francés* on the southern side of the Cantabrians, others arrived by ship in the northern ports and then proceeded overland. From this northern region came many of the *hidalgos* who migrated to the more southerly parts of the kingdom and founded great estates.

Just south of the northern coastal region lies the northern Meseta, covering most of Old Castile and much of the old kingdom of León. Bounded in the north by the Cantabrian and Asturian chains and in the south by the Sierra de Gredos and the Sierra de Guadarrama, this had been the first area reconquered from the Muslims, and in the early period the labor shortage had allowed the peasants to secure land with favorable conditions of tenure. Their most important advantage was the ability to establish *behetrías*, townships whose inhabitants had the right of choosing their lords. This had lasted until the fourteenth century, but with the rise of the aristocracy the land was rapidly converted into a mosaic of seigneurial estates. It was a rich section, producing wheat and grapes and providing seasonal pasturage for the transhumant herds of sheep. Burgos—seat of the association of wool merchants, Medina del Campo—with its famous fairs, and Segovia, a textile producer, were important financial centers; along with Avila and Valladolid they were the scene of many of the political squabbles of Enrique's reign.

South of the Guadarramas was the southern Meseta, a region where the economic keynote was pastoralism. It offered winter grazing for transhumant sheep, and, with Andalusia, it was virtually the only European area where large-scale cattle ranching existed.[2] Mainly an area of large landholdings, in the course of the fifteenth century aristocratic families were engaged in securing control of the cities so as to gain political and economic leverage. Madrid was small but important because of royal patronage; Enrique loved to hunt in the nearby woods of El Pardo. Toledo was wracked by constant social upheavals, while Guadalajara was in the hands of the

2. Bishko, "Cattle Ranching," pp. 494–501.

Mendoza family. In the lower part of the southern Meseta the military orders of Calatrava, Alcántara, and Santiago had formed virtually independent kingdoms as a result of the reconquest.

Finally there was the south—Murcia and Andalusia—dominated by the valley of the Guadalquivir. Most recently reconquered, it still contained some Mudéjares (Muslims living under Christian rule). There was sheep grazing, but cattle raising and agriculture were more important. Vineyards, olive orchards, and irrigated truck gardens brought the area its real wealth. As in the southern Meseta, most of the land was divided into large estates. Along the lower reaches of the Guadalquivir was the complex of ports which made up the economic nucleus of the south of the kingdom—Seville, a large and variegated city, San Lúcar de Barrameda, and Cádiz. The ports were important for exports of Castilian products and the import and transshipment of goods from northern Europe and the Mediterranean. Finance was influenced by Italian merchants, Genoese and Florentines, who also served as intermediaries for the trade in gold from Africa.[3]

Still in the hands of the Muslims, the kingdom of Granada covered the mountainous territories bounded by the city of Granada, Málaga, and Gibraltar. Ringed by Castilian frontier fortresses, it was important to Castile for a small amount of trade, for the tribute its rulers paid to Castile, and for the booty which could be seized in Castilian raids. The failure of Enrique IV to prosecute vigorously the war against Granada was to cause him grave political difficulty.

The first step in the Castilian march of overseas conquest had been undertaken in Africa and the Canaries. In the last years of the fourteenth century, Castilians, in particular men from the Basque provinces and Andalusia, had begun to compete with the Portuguese for the goods of West Africa—gold, slaves, spices, marble, dyes—which had previously reached Europe via Muslim traders. Operating directly from the peninsula or from bases in the Canaries, Castilians made raids along the African coast.[4] The Castilian hold on the Canaries had begun earlier, and by the reign of Enrique IV Castilian nobles controlled the smaller islands. In 1468 Enrique named

3. Florentino Pérez-Embid, "Navigation et commerce dans le port de Séville au bas moyen âge," *Moyen Age*, no. 3-4 (1969):263–89, 479–502; Jacques Heers, *Gênes au XVe siècle: Activité économique et problèmes sociaux* (Paris, 1961); and Jacques Heers, *L'Occident aux XIVe et XVe siècles: Aspects économiques et sociaux*, 2nd. ed. (Paris, 1966), pp. 171–72, 203.

4. Antonio Rumeu de Armas, *España en el Africa atlántica*, 2 vols. (Madrid, 1956-57), 1:32, 49, 91–92.

Diego García de Herrera as lord of the Canaries and the African coast, with overlordship reserved for the Castilian crown and church affairs for the archbishop of Seville.[5] The king endangered the attempted Castilian monopoly in the Canaries by allowing certain Portuguese nobles to participate in the conquest of uncontrolled areas, but he later reversed this policy.

For Castile as a whole, fishing, forestry, mining, and cattle were important, but the real wealth of the kingdom came from wool. The export economy was vitally dependent on it in this period. The expanding European market for wool in the late Middle Ages meant that centers for the absorption of raw wool, especially the new draperies in Italy and Flanders, vigorously sought Castilian exports. When English wool production suffered a decline in the fourteenth century, Castile was in an excellent position to fill the market. The introduction of the Merino sheep from Africa, possibly through the influence of Genoese merchants, gave the country a growing supply of fine wool from hearty flocks. By 1400 Castile had cornered the international market for wool. In Flanders, both for consumption there and transshipment to central Europe, wool from the peninsula was replacing English wool, and Castile at times even sent wool to England. Because of this phenomenal growth, wool production and trade became the single most important element in the economy. Flocks of sheep covered the Castilian hills, and peasant farmers, especially after the devastation of the Black Death in the mid-fourteenth century, were unable to resist the encroachment of the sheepherders and the Mesta, the powerful association of sheep flock owners.[6]

Late in the Middle Ages Castile generally exchanged the raw or semifinished materials of its mines, fields, and pastures for the manufactured goods and luxury products of the regions with which it traded. In its economy foreign merchants were often vitally important, but we must recognize the commitment to trade of many native Castilians. Castile was not exclusively a land of saints and soldiers. Basque and Castilian seamen ranged along the Atlantic and Mediterranean coasts of Europe. Andalusian nobles co-operated with the Italians and engaged in commerce on their own. The greatest landowners of the kingdom—the lords of the Mesta—felt a vital

5. Enrique IV, confirmation made in Palencia, 6 April 1468, printed in Rumeu, *España en el Africa atlántica*, 2:4; Richard Konetzke, *El imperio español: Orígenes y fundamentos*, trans. Felipe González Vicén (Madrid, 1946), pp. 40, 106-110.

6. Vicens, *Economic History of Spain*, pp. 250-52; Robert S. Lopez, "El origen de la oveja merina," *Estudios de historia moderna* 4 (1954):1-13; Julius Klein, *The Mesta: A Study in Spanish Economic History, 1273-1836* (Cambridge, Mass., 1920).

concern for the tides of economic fortune as they negotiated with the long-distance merchants of Burgos and other cities, who sold wool in the manufacturing regions and brought back to Castile the luxury products they obtained there. Major industrial activity in textiles, metal work, and shipbuilding was certainly beginning, along with a host of minor industries. Although exploitation of the soil and subsoil was the pre-eminent economic mode, we cannot overlook the highly developed commercial urge of many Castilians.

The crisis in Castile, already under way by the reign of Juan II and reaching its height in the reign of his son Enrique IV, was not caused primarily by economic concerns. Rather it was due to a complex set of overlapping and interrelated factors: the aggressive assertion of power on the part of the nobility, the increasingly hostile relations among the three religions of the peninsula, and the inability of the monarchy to exercise its traditional leadership. The key to the political events of fifteenth-century Castilian history is the dramatic series of confrontations between members of the high nobility and the monarchy. The lowest rung of the three-fold division of the nobility was occupied by the *hidalgos*, whose only advantages were a certain degree of social prestige and exemption from ordinary taxation. Above them were lords (*señores*) with small territorial possessions (*señoríos*). The *títulos* were the titled nobility of *grandes* at the top of the scale. The counts, marquises, and dukes were wealthy and powerful, and their wealth and power were increasing. As their love of luxury and display grew, they erected fortresses and palatial urban houses, and most of the imports into Castile—especially fine cloth—were destined solely for them. Patronized by the nobility, the fair of Medina del Campo was during the century probably Europe's most important luxury market.[7]

The late flowering of the Castilian *grandes*, who were identified as such in the Cortes of 1451, deserves explanation. It was a new nobility. Most of the old noble houses had died out in the fourteenth century and had been replaced by aggressive new lines.[8] The European crisis of the mid-fourteenth century was coupled in Castile with a devastating civil war between two sons of Alfonso XI. Victorious in the conflict was Enrique de

7. Santiago Sobrequés Vidal, "La época del patriciado urbano," in vol. 2 of *Historia social y económica de España y América*, ed. Jaime Vicens Vives (Barcelona, 1957), pp. 111–30, has an excellent discussion of the high nobility.

8. Salvador de Moxó, "De la nobleza vieja a la nobleza nueva: La transformación nobiliaria castellana en la baja Edad Media," *Cuadernos de Historia* 3 (Madrid, 1969).

Trastámara, the standard bearer of the noble faction. Since so many noble families had been killed off, Enrique II and his Trastámara successors were in a position to reward their followers with lavish grants of land and titles. The crown could do so because of the existence of vast tracts of under-populated lands in the south—in Murcia, Extremadura, La Mancha, and Andalusia. The area had been reconquered in the thirteenth century, and it was easily suited to latifundia and exploitation by grazing.

The holdings of the *grandes* were scattered. The greatest of them had towns and lands in several provinces. While they typically had a favored stronghold and various other fortresses, they did not usually reside on their estates. Their sphere of action was rather the major towns and cities and, in the case of the greatest nobles, the royal court. In the towns and cities they moved to dominate the municipal governments and judicial positions by establishing links of kinship and patronage with families of the lesser nobility to enhance their political and economic pre-eminence. In the royal court they sought to establish hereditary control over important royal offices, such as the admiralty of Castile; they exerted great leverage on foreign commerce and over the high positions of the Mesta. With their insertion into the highest levels of the royal government they could secure influence and grants for themselves.

The aristocratic establishment was not closed; movement in and out of its ranks was common. Weaknesses of the Trastámara kings allowed noble aggrandizement. Enrique II (1369-79) had to reward the nobles who helped him to power with extensive grants known as the "mercedes enriqueñas." Juan I (1379-90) faced war with the Portuguese and English and therefore had to continue to favor the aristocracy in return for their military support. Relatively weak or divided regencies during the minorities of Enrique III and Juan II allowed the nobles to continue their rise to power. They were successful in establishing entailed estates (*mayorazgos*), impossible earlier in Castile, but increasingly possible and common in the fourteenth and fifteenth centuries.

Vastly more wealthy and influential than any single noble family were the great Castilian military orders: Calatrava, Alcántara, and Santiago. These brotherhoods had been founded in the second half of the twelth century. Vitally helpful to the Castilian kings in the reconquest of the south, the orders received huge land grants in Extremadura, La Mancha, and on the frontier of Granada. These grants included rich pasture lands eminently suitable for sheep grazing, and as a result the masters of the orders were intimately involved in the Mesta. Possessing a population of vassals numbering around one million, the masters of the three orders controlled revenues of over forty thousand ducats per year. Together the grand masters had the privilege of bestowing nobility on some fifteen hundred individuals, who could be made knights of the orders or appointed to the more exalted office of commander. The orders offered respected and influential positions for the minor nobles and the younger sons of the great families. Their wealth and power made the orders potential threats to the crown, and one of the most important moves made by Fernando and Isabel was to assert a stringent royal control over them.[9] Enrique IV anticipated the Catholic Monarchs in this policy.

By the mid-fifteenth century and the time of Enrique's succession, less than a score of great families had amassed vast amounts of lands, titles, wealth, and political positions.[10] The wealth of the high nobility rested on a common economic base—the land and the produce of that land. Whether they raised wheat, wine grapes, or olives, or whether they derived their income from wool and hides from their sheep and cattle herds, the primary desire was to secure the greatest possible return from their agricultural and pastoral pursuits. Ownership of fisheries—as in the case of the Guzmanes—was analogous. The export trade—control of ports for the income they could produce or the direct ownership of shipping—was their economic vehicle. In general, the aristocracy was concerned with the production of basic commodities and the export of those commodities. In contrast, royal policy under Enrique IV offered a challenge to Castile's traditional economic orientation. On a minor scale, his attempt to create a rival commer-

9. Vicens, *Economic History of Spain*, pp. 161, 167.

10. Except as otherwise noted, the following discussion of the individual great noble families comes from Suárez, "Los Trastámaras," pp. 16-22, and Roger Highfield, "The Catholic Kings and the Titled Nobility of Castile," in *Europe in the Late Middle Ages*, ed. John Hale, J.R.L. Highfield, and Beryl Smalley (London, 1965), pp. 358-85, which is more restricted in time than the author fully acknowledges. For the dates of their titles, Lowell W. Newton, "The Development of the Castilian Peerage" (unpublished Ph. D. dissertation, Tulane University, 1972), pp. 215, 240-41. The information concerning their titles comes from the records at AGS, *Quitaciones de Corte*, particularly *legs*. 1-4. Royal grants are found in RAH, *Salazar*; AHN, *Osuna*; and AGS, *Mercedes y privilegios*.

María Isabel del Val Valdivieso, "Los bandos nobiliarios durante el reinado de Enrique IV," *Hispania* 35 (1975):249-93, provides a discussion of the nobles, but her work is marred by the attempt to force her data into the monarchist or anti-monarchist mold. She follows the typology of Luis Suárez Fernández, her mentor at the University of Valladolid, too closely.

cial fair in his own city of Segovia was a threat to the noble fairs. But more important, his legislation of 1462 to retain in the kingdom one-third of all raw wool for use by the embryonic weaving industry was a severe threat to the lords of the Mesta. It was likely a secondary cause of the rebellion of two years later.

The political and economic resources of the aristocracy were intricately mingled. Another important source of wealth came from political rewards, both for loyal service (particularly in time of war) and for promises of loyalty. The king had at his disposal a vast array of material to award as *mercedes* (gifts); for a variety of reasons discussed later, Enrique made lavish use of his power to grant. Royal offices, both in the central government and in the provinces and cities, were lucrative gifts, offering salaries and the potential for graft. Titles, mostly with more honorific than real significance, were bestowed. Outright monetary grants and gifts of vassals, gifts of towns and villages, rights to found *mayorazgos* (entailed estates) were offered and gladly received. Perhaps most devastating for the fiscal position of the crown were Enrique's grants of income based upon royal taxes and customs revenues. We will see specific examples of all these rewards as we proceed.

Probably the most influential aristocratic family in the period was that of the Mendozas. They controlled a number of towns in an area bounded on the north by the modern province of Santander, on the south by Guadalajara, and stretching east from Madrid to Soria. In 1445 Iñigo López de Mendoza, the family's leader, gained the titles of marquis of Santillana and count of El Real de Manzanares because of his support of Juan II in the first battle of Olmedo. He died in 1458, leaving six sons well entrenched in the affairs of the kingdom. The chief possessions passed to Diego Hurtado de Mendoza, second marquis of Santillana. In 1467, Iñigo López, namesake of the first marquis, became count of Tendilla, and Lorenzo Suárez de Figueroa—given an old family name—got the title of count of La Coruña del Conde (in the modern province of Burgos). These titles, and other concessions made at the same time, were rewards for loyalty as the civil war began. While not *grandes*, two other sons were Juan, lord of Fresno de Torete, and Hurtado, who held various royal appointments. Of the six brothers, Pedro González de Mendoza, whose significant titles were clerical rather than secular, was closest to the ruler. Pedro González moved steadily through a succession of episcopal sees, finishing his career as the "Cardinal of Spain." He was one of the most astute politicians of the period, forming a Mendoza family alliance with the king in the early 1460s—

with consequent grants—and constantly opposing the Pacheco faction. While he came to favor the succession of Isabel, he never broke with Enrique.[11]

A vastly influential family was composed of the Acuñas, Pachecos, Girones, and Portocarreros. Of Portuguese ancestry, branches of the family took the names of the Castilian lines they married into. The most prominent member was Alfonso Carrillo de Acuña, archbishop of Toledo and primate of Spain. Pedro de Acuña, who was named count of Buendía in the last year of Enrique's reign, held the vital position of chief officer of the Mesta, which remained in the family well into the Habsburg period.[12] Responsible for many of the political intrigues of Enrique's times, the brothers Juan Pacheco and Pedro Girón (Archbishop Carrillo's nephews) became Enrique's closest advisors while he was prince and remained near at hand thereafter.

The Enríquez family, with holdings in Old Castile in the modern provinces of Palencia and Valladolid, was one of the kingdom's most prominent. There were two main branches of the family: Fadrique Enríquez, hereditary admiral of Castile, was head of the major branch, while Enrique Enríquez, count of Alba de Liste, led the minor branch. Their possession of Medina de Ríoseco with its commercial fair and the admiral's interest in trade meant that they favored the traditional Castilian economic orientation toward export of primary materials and the import of luxuries. The marriage of Juana Enríquez, the admiral's daughter, with the future Juan II of Aragon, forged an indissoluble bond between the family and the Aragonese.

In the northeast of the kingdom lay the lands of the Velasco family, counts of Haro since 1430. With possessions covering much of the present-day provinces of Burgos and Logroño, the count of Haro (Pedro Fernández de Velasco in Enrique's time) controlled the important routes between Burgos and Bilbao, through which passed the bulk of Castilian wool ship-

11. Francisco Layna Serrano, *Historia de Guadalajara y sus Mendozas en los siglos XV y XVI*, 4 vols. (Madrid, 1942), 2:9, 22–24, 30–39, 75–76. Our knowledge of the Mendoza family will be immeasurably expanded when Professor Helen Nader of Indiana University publishes her major study. I am grateful to her for the correct date of the Tendilla title; the printed sources say 1465.

12. Various copies of Enrique IV's grants of this office are in RAH, *Salazar*, *leg.* D-13, fols. 86–89; *leg.* M-5, fol. 272; *leg.* M-27, fols. 251v–253v. In 1465 Enrique gave the Acuña family perpetual control, ibid., *leg.* M-27, fol. 260v. In January 1568 the sixth count of Buendía, Juan de Acuña, renounced the office in favor of the crown, but whether the renunciation was permanent is in question since Felipe III reconfirmed the office (ibid.). For the *Reyes Católicos'* confirmation, RAH, *Salazar*, *leg.* M-27, fols. 254v–56.

ments on their way to the weaving centers of France and Flanders, and the customs dues, the *diezmos de la mar*.

The Pimentel family controlled an important region in the kingdom of León, centering on the town of Benavente, from which they took their most important title. The Manriques controlled part of the *tierra de campos* from Palencia north to Reinosa. Possessing five comptal titles—Castañeda, Paredes de Nava, Treviño, Ribadeo, and Osorno—at the beginning of Enrique's reign, they formed a powerful bloc which usually opposed the king. Allied with the Mendozas, the family of la Cerda, led by Juan de la Cerda (count of Medinaceli), owned lands in Soria and Guadalajara provinces. The town of Medinaceli was the hub of their possessions, but they had interests in the ports of Andalusia and were shipowners in their own right. The Quiñones dominated the borderlands of León and Asturias. Headed by Diego Fernández de Quiñones, count of Luna, the family achieved great power because of their early support of Isabel.

Control of Galicia was the persistent dream of the counts of Trastámara. In 1445 Juan II awarded the title to Pedro Alvarez de Osorio, who additionally gained the title of count of Villalobos. His kinsman, Alvaro Pérez de Osorio, became marquis of Astorga in 1465 and served as a *guarda mayor* and *alférez* for Enrique IV. Often isolated from the national political scene, Galicia was wracked by the struggles between the Osorios and the archbishops of Santiago.

On the Portuguese frontier in the south of the kingdom of León and throughout Extremadura lay the holdings of several noble families. One was the Alvarez de Toledo. Juan II created Fernand Alvarez de Toledo count of Alba de Tormes in 1430. He was succeeded in 1465 by García Alvarez de Toledo, who became marquis of Coria in 1469. With lands along the paths of transhumance, the family derived much of its wealth from the sheep flocks.

With an arc of territories stretching from Burgos to Cáceres, a more influential family in the western grazing region was the Stúñiga (occasionally spelled Estúñiga in the fifteenth century and generally spelled Zúñiga from the sixteenth). Pedro de Stúñiga became count of Plasencia during Juan II's reign; his grandson Alvaro de Stúñiga was a powerful figure in the reign of Enrique IV.

In the south three powerful families dominated the political and economic landscape. In the east, the Fajardos enjoyed virtual independence in the kingdom of Murcia—a clear example of how clever politicians could convert royal posts into independent possessions. In 1383 Alfonso Yáñez

Fajardo became *adelantado mayor* of Murcia; four years later he gained the small town of Alhama. By 1465 the Fajardos had expanded their lands and titles so steadily that Pedro Fajardo, while still legally subject to the king as *adelantado mayor*, was able to act as uncrowned ruler of the entire region, completely uncontrolled by the court.[13]

Two of the kingdom's most powerful families operated in western Andalusia: the Ponces de León and the Guzmanes. The first held lands in the modern provinces of Seville and Cádiz, including the port of Cádiz. Pedro Ponce de León attained the title of count of Medellín in 1429 and in 1440 that of count of Arcos de la Frontera. In the 1460s the second count of Arcos, Rodrigo Ponce de León became marquis of Cádiz. Because of their port holdings they were extremely active in sea trade and invested in shipping.[14]

The Guzmán family were deadly rivals of the Ponces de León. With lands in the provinces of Huelva, Seville, and Cádiz, they controlled numerous towns, most importantly the port of San Lúcar de Barrameda, and regarded Seville as their personal fief. In 1462 Juan de Guzmán, count of Niebla and duke of Medina-Sidonia, conquered Gibraltar. Considerable confusion over title to the small but important territory ensued, but by 1468 Juan's successor Enrique de Guzmán secured title to it. Besides territorial holdings, the Guzmanes' sources of wealth were varied and lucrative. They were wine producers and exporters; they controlled tuna fisheries; they were shipowners.[15]

Throughout his reign Enrique IV had to struggle against opposition from some of these noble clans. Luis Suárez Fernández, whose work has already been discussed in the first chapter, suggests a constitutional conflict to account for the unrest, postulating a two-fold division of the nobility—monarchists and anti-monarchists—and, somewhat contradictorily, the existence of a holistic noble oligarchy.[16] Suárez believes that the nobility wanted to reduce the king to a figurehead, and while he states in the second edition of *Nobleza y monarquía* that no one wanted to abolish the monarchy, he still implies that the nobles wanted a constitutional

13. Juan Torres Fontes, *Fajardo el Bravo* (Murcia, 1944) and by the same author, *Don Pedro Fajardo, adelantado de Murcia* (Madrid, 1953).

14. Richard Konetzke, "Entrepreneurial Activities of Spanish and Portuguese Noblemen in Medieval Times," *Explorations in Entrepreneurial History* 6 (1953):116.

15. Ibid.; J.L. Cano de Gardoqui and A. de Bethencourt, "Incorporación de Gibraltar a la corona de Castilla (1436-1508)," *Hispania* 26 (1966):324-81.

16. See the discussion of Suárez's interpretation in the first chapter, pp. 11-13 and notes 27-30.

change. The noble class as a whole, he tells us, "had its own political concept . . . whose consequences we cannot measure because the victory of their aspirations was never fully realized."[17] One significant objection to Suárez's interpretation was that it is impossible to lump all the nobles together and speak of class interests or a class view shared by all. Their aims were always particularistic, and if at times we can identify temporary alliances of monarchists or anti-monarchists, their rosters were never stable since members shifted in and out according to the dictates of circumstance.

Was there a revolutionary or even a constitutional crisis? The Sentence of Medina del Campo in 1465, to be considered at length in the fifth chapter, would have given a committee chosen by the dissidents great power to share in and shape royal decisions. Even the mild Enrique IV went to war rather than agree to the demands, and his resolve was backed by the arms of his own noble followers. There was only one attempt in fifteenth-century Castile to establish a political arrangement outside the bounds of the traditional monarchy. This was in 1433 when Fadrique de Aragón (the grandson of the Aragonese king Martín I) mounted a quickly quashed effort to establish an independent Seville on the model of the Italian city republics.[18] All the nobles really wanted was a monarch whom they could influence; when they rebelled they could think of no other course than to create a rival king.

Even without a revolutionary challenge, there was constant tension between the crown and the nobles, and it can be demonstrated that the political history of Castile in the last phase of the Middle Ages was a result of that tension. There was no other group powerful enough to mount more than a local challenge. Between them, the crown and the nobility had checked political expression of other groups. The Cortes, the parliamentary body, was more democratic earlier, but by the fifteenth century it was weak and unrepresentative. Only certain cities were represented, and the delegates were often appointed, designated, and influenced by either the king or the local nobility. The urban representatives to the Cortes were usually *hidalgos*, linked to the nobles, not the commoners. Many urban centers were controlled by the crown or aristocrats via alliances with lesser nobles active at the local levels.

If the nobles were the only politically active group, how can we account for their activities if not on constitutional grounds? A simple ex-

17. Suárez, "Los Trastámaras," p. 22.

18. Miguel Angel Ladero Quesada, *Andalucía en el siglo XV: Estudios de historia política* (Madrid, 1973), p. 103.

planation seems to satisfy all the requirements. The nobles who allied with one another, sought Aragonese aid, or raised rival kings were motivated by a series of pragmatic urges. Family links, particularly exemplified by the ties of the Enríquez family with the Aragonese crown, were in operation, as were traditional antagonisms between families. More important were perceptions of their own good. If royal grants of various kinds—monetary, territorial, of crown taxes—were important sources of noble revenue, what better way to gain grants than by stirring up trouble? Local revolts could be raised and revenue-producing positions or taxes seized. Then, to reward their return to loyalty, the grateful monarch might give legal sanction to the usurpations. If rewards could not be gained from the existing monarch, a rival king—*de facto* or *de jure*— could be created, as was the case in certain periods in Enrique's revolts against his father and Alvaro de Luna, and more particularly in the case of the coronation of Enrique's half brother Alfonso as king. To end these rebellions, or threats of rebellion, the king would often allow repentant nobles to keep their gains. This also explains why the battles are seldom large and never decisive. When civil war did break out, there was no sectional or class conflict. Rather, simmering local conflicts—over control of a city, frontier fortress, or territory—came to the boil, as the antagonists took advantage of royal preoccupations elsewhere.

Ideology played no part in the program of the nobles, nor was conflict between classes of primary importance. The nobles did move to take control of towns from non-nobles, but far more significant were the nobles' contests with one another or with the crown. Economic concerns were certainly present. The nobles maintained and enhanced their economic position, but this was a consequence of their political actions, not because they had radically new economic perspectives. The events of Enrique's tenure as crown prince and as king will allow us to test this explanation and trace the relations between the crown and the aristocracy.

III

PRINCE OF ASTURIAS

Enrique IV, the fifth Castilian king of the house of Trastámara, was to take the throne at a singularly disordered period in peninsular affairs. The roots of the unrest went back to the days of the founder of the dynasty, Enrique of Trastámara, one of five bastard sons of Alfonso XI (1312-50). Alfonso's only legitimate son was Pedro I, who was able to rule for nineteen years after the death of his father, despite heavy opposition. Enrique fought vigorously against his half brother, rallying Castilian support and bringing in foreign intervention in the form of the famous White Companies under Bernard du Guesclin. Pedro, popularly known as Pedro the Cruel, secured the help of the Black Prince and his English troops and defeated Guesclin's forces at Nájera. Finally, in 1369, Pedro was murdered during an interview with Enrique at Montiel.

The new king, Enrique II (1369-79), was the victor in a civil war which had much wider implications than a mere struggle between half brothers. In the traditional view of historians, the middle classes had supported Pedro, while Enrique's followers had exemplified the aristocratic reaction. While true in general terms, this dichotomy is overdrawn. No king of the period would have wished to abolish or even seriously curtail the noble estate, and because long-distance trade occupied a vital place in the Castilian economy, no king could seriously threaten the merchants. Enrique of Trastámara exploited growing religious antagonisms in his campaign against Pedro, and older historians saw this as an attack on both Jews and the middle class. Once he gained the throne, however, he toned down his religious policy. He did favor the nobility, as did his successors, but this in large measure was due to the weakening of the nobility, many of whose members died out through natural causes or in the civil war, leaving their titles vacant and their lands available for the king's disposition. Not surprisingly, the first Trastámara liberally rewarded those who had supported him. Enrique II faced the possibility of war with Aragon, Navarre, Portugal, and England, so the flow of grants continued throughout his reign. A newly created nobility had come into prominence and was not timid about asserting its strength.[1]

The successors of Enrique II continued to favor the aristocracy in return for noble assistance and good will. As mentioned in the previous chapter, the new nobles sought to expand and protect their positions by turning their public offices into hereditary sinecures. Juan I (1379-90) devoted most of his energies to foreign concerns. His second marriage was with the daughter of the last Portuguese king of the house of Burgundy. When his father-in-law died in 1383, Juan I attempted to assume the Portuguese throne. Portuguese popular sentiment rallied behind the bastard João de Avis, who successfully claimed the Portuguese throne and destroyed the Castilian invasion army at Aljubarrota in 1385. Before Juan had time to recover, John of Gaunt, the duke of Lancaster, brought in an English army to press the claims of his wife Constance, an illegitimate daughter of Pedro the Cruel, to the Castilian throne. A compromise eventually calmed the dispute: the English recognized the legality of the Trastámara possession of the Castilian crown in return for the marriage of John of Gaunt's daughter, Catherine of Lancaster, with the Castilian heir, the future Enrique III. Earlier, John of Gaunt had married another daughter, Philippa, to João de Avis.[2]

Enrique III proved to be an able ruler, even though his short reign (1390-1406) was further reduced by a three-year regency at its beginning. Like Juan I, his main concern was the pursuit of a vigorous foreign policy. He entered the Castilian naval forces in the struggle for control of the western Mediterranean and renewed the war against Granada. During his reign Castilian emissaries went as far east as the court of Tamerlane, and far enough west to begin the conquest of the Canaries (1402).

The death of Enrique III in 1406 brought a new actor onto the stage of Castilian politics: Fernando de Antequera. The new king Juan II (1406-54) was a minor, and the dead king's will left the regency jointly to his wife Catherine and his younger brother Fernando. The young king's uncle, soon

1. For an introduction to fourteenth-century Castilian politics, see Julio Valdeón Baruque, *Enrique II de Castilla: La guerra civil y la consolidación del régimen (1366-1371)* (Valladolid, 1966) and Joaquín Gimeno Casalduero, *La imagen del monarca en la Castilla del siglo XIV: Pedro el Cruel, Enrique II, y Juan I* (Madrid, 1972). For the nobility, see Salvador de Moxó, "De la nobleza vieja a la nobleza nueva: La transformación nobiliaria castellana en la baja Edad Media," *Cuadernos de Historia* 3 (Madrid, 1969).

2. The standard work on Juan I is that of Luis Suárez Fernández, *Juan I, Rey de Castilla (1379-1390)* (Madrid, 1955).

to gain the appellation "de Antequera" as a result of his victory there over the Muslims of Granada, was extremely powerful in his own right. His possessions included the strategic towns of Medina del Campo, Olmedo, Cuéllar, and Villalón. In addition, through his wife Leonor, daughter of the count of Alburquerque, he controlled Haro, Ledesma, and Alburquerque. In 1410 the Aragonese throne fell vacant without a clear claimant. By the Compromise of Caspe in 1412, nine arbiters chosen by the Cortes of the kingdoms of the Crown of Aragon offered Fernando the Aragonese throne.[3]

For the last four years of his life (1412-16) Fernando de Antequera was both king of Aragon and regent of Castile. He lost no interest in Castilian affairs despite his elevation to the new position. Instead, through his sons and daughter, he consolidated his influence over Castile. His eldest son, Alfonso, was the Aragonese heir. The second son, Juan, had Castilian holdings consisting of Peñafiel, Lara, and Mayorga. By marrying Blanca de Navarra, Juan secured control of that kingdom. Enrique, Fernando's third son, was master of Santiago and count of Alburquerque, his maternal inheritance. Sancho was made master of Alcántara, while young Pedro was to play an important role later. María became the wife of Juan II of Castile. The Infantes of Aragon, as Fernando's offspring were known, gave their name to a significant epoch in Castilian history.[4]

Most of Juan II's reign, from the time he attained his majority in 1419 to his death in 1454, was a constant struggle to reduce the Infantes' strangle hold on Castile. His greatest support was Alvaro de Luna, an able statesman who fully understood the danger to the monarchy posed by the Infantes and who engineered their ultimate downfall. Unfortunately, the personal and political qualities of Juan II and Alvaro de Luna, while successful in asserting a minimal control over the kingdom, were such as to weaken support for the monarchical institution. A mild, well-educated man who knew Latin, Juan was psychologically unsuited to governing and preferred to indulge his affinities for hunting and literary pursuits. He delegated all power to Luna, who gained such control that nothing was done without his approval. According to the contemporary chronicler, Fernán Pérez de Guzmán, some felt that Luna had bewitched the king. Though Pérez did not accept the idea of bewitchment, he did say that

> Never one single hour did the king wish to engage in or work at ruling, although in his time there were . . . so many revolts and movements,

3. I.I. MacDonald, *Don Fernando de Antequera* (Oxford, 1948).
4. Eloy Benito Ruano, *Los infantes de Aragón* (Madrid, 1952).

and injuries, and evils and dangers as there had not been for the space of two hundred years, from which to his person and fame and kingdom came abundant danger.[5]

Alvaro de Luna, a bastard nephew of the archibishop of Toledo Pedro de Luna, was physically small but exceedingly skilled and persuasive in debate. He worked constantly to maintain and enhance the power of the monarchy. The author of the *Crónica de Alvaro de Luna* called him "certainly the best knight there was in his time in all the Spains," and reported that Luna showed his commitment to the monarchy by acting as "the principal guide and director of the events of the kingdom, in all the tempests and storms which were raised and took place in it."[6] But Luna's motive was not pure loyalty. Everything he did was also directed toward his personal advantage.[7]

To explain Juan's reliance on Luna, the chronicler Alvar García de Santa María suggested that it stemmed from a time when the king was a child and Luna was an impressive adolescent in the court. Juan, whose father was dead, was governed by antagonistic regents—his mother and uncle—and seems to have turned to Luna as a constant figure in a turbulent world. As Juan's reign unfolded, and Luna's consistent support became apparent, Juan rewarded him with great concessions, much to the annoyance of the *grandes*.[8]

Six years after Juan II was recognized as of age, his wife María of Aragon gave birth to a son and heir: Enrique, who was born either the fifth or sixth of January 1425, in the Valladolid home of Diego Sánchez, Juan II's *contador mayor de cuentas*. Alvaro de Luna acted as his godfather. The following April (on the twenty-first) Juan installed Enrique as prince of Asturias, heir to the kingdoms of the crown of Castile.[9] Little is known of

5. Fernán Pérez de Guzmán, *Generaciones y semblanzas*, ed. R.B. Tate (London, (1965), pp. 39–41. Pérez seems to have forgotten the Trastámara revolution of the fourteenth century.

6. *Crónica de Don Alvaro de Luna: Condestable de Castilla, Maestre de Santiago*, ed. Juan de Mata Carriazo, Colección de crónicas españoles 2 (Madrid, 1940), pp. 287, 298.

7. Pérez, *Generaciones y semblanzas*, pp. 44–45. Alvaro de Luna gained the important title of constable in 1423, RAH, *Salazar*, *leg*. M-9, fols. 272–274v.

8. Alvar García de Santa María, *Crónica de Don Juan II de Castilla, años 1420-1434*, in vols. 99–100 of *Codoin*, 100:302–304.

9. *Crónica de Alvaro de Luna*, p. 54; García, *Crónica de Juan II*, in *Codoin*, 99:345; Pedro Carrillo de Huete, *Crónica del halconero de Juan II*, ed. Juan de Mata Carriazo, Colección de crónicas españoles 8 (Madrid, 1946), p. 9; Lope Barrientos, *Refundición de la Crónica del halconero*, ed. Juan de Mata Carriazo, Colección de

his early years, unfortunately for psycho-historical analysis. Bishop Lope Barrientos was his principal tutor. The chronicles present a tender scene in 1431 when Barrientos saved the life of the six-year-old prince by carrying him from a threatened tower in Madrid in the midst of an earthquake.[10] Officially, care and protection of the young Enrique were provided by his *ayo* Pedro Fernández de Córdoba, lord of Baena, who died in 1435. Thereafter Juan II entrusted the heir to Alvaro de Luna. Juan's powerful favorite turned actual charge of the prince over to three men: Juan de Cerenzuela, Alvaro de Luna's brother and archbishop of Toledo; Ruy Díaz de Mendoza, Juan's *mayordomo mayor*; and a knight from Seville, Pedro Manuel. At the same time Luna introduced Juan Pacheco into the train of the prince.[11] Pacheco later became Enrique's chief confidant for most of the crucial periods of his life, and in his last years Alvaro de Luna found Pacheco one of his chief rivals.

In 1436 Juan II began negotiations for the marriage of his son with Blanca de Navarra. The marriage ceremony took place four years later—15 September 1440 in Valladolid. As the daughter of Juan, the most persistent and feared of the Infantes of Aragon, Blanca (who had the same name as her mother) provided her father with a potential weapon for use against the Castilian monarchy. From the time of his marriage, as the chronicles assert, Enrique fell increasingly under the influence of Juan Pacheco. This consummate politician apparently tried to secure the same influence over Enrique as Alvaro de Luna had over the king. During the months that preceded Enrique's marriage, a series of obscure political maneuvers were in progress. Probably urged on by Pacheco, Enrique insisted on and secured a personal household and obtained control of the city of Segovia. In June 1440 an Aragonese entourage headed by Juan of Navarre was in Castile, with the dissident Castilian nobles gravitating around it. With little warning

crónicas españoles 9 (Madrid, 1946), p. 47. Since the late fourteenth century the heir to the Castilian throne had been invested with the lordship of Asturias, from whence he took his title, and with various towns in Andalusia. See Luis G. de Valdeavellano, *Curso de historia de las instituciones españoles de los orígenes al final de la Edad Media*, 4th ed. (Madrid, 1975), p. 438.

10. Carrillo, *Crónica del halconero*, p. 92; Barrientos, *Refundición*, p. 115.

11. *Crónica de Alvaro de Luna*, p. 147; Barrientos, *Refundición*, pp. 196–97. In 1432 the master of Alcántara, Gutierre de Sotomayor, turned over his position as Enrique's *guarda mayor* to Gonzalo Sánchez Topete: RAH, *Salazar*, *leg.* M-173, *hojas* 92–93. For notes on the Fernández de Córdoba family's control of the office of *ayo*, see Miguel Angel Ladero Quesada, *Andalucía en el siglo XV: Estudios de historia política* (Madrid, 1973), pp. 48, 102.

Enrique left his father and sought refuge with Juan of Navarre. When pressed for an explanation, the prince of Asturias stated that he distrusted a number of his father's courtiers. Since he did not wish to jeopardize the marriage of his daughter, Juan of Navarre urged Enrique to return to his father's side, and after two courtiers were expelled, the prince did so.[12]

An explanation for these machinations is not easily provided. There was undoubtedly trouble between Juan of Castile and his queen. Before 1440 the queen and her son were constantly at the king's side on state occasions; thereafter they were to be generally absent. Perhaps the queen influenced her son, perhaps the fifteen-year-old prince was not yet ready for marriage, or perhaps Pacheco used Enrique's indecision to his own advantage. Although his view is no doubt oversimplified, the chronicler Pedro Carrillo de Huete was clear about the force moving Enrique.

> Juan Pacheco turned him from the opinion and obedience of the lord king his father, and he himself managed the reconciliation. And he did this since he wanted to gain from the king some large gifts and grants; and with this technique he gained and advanced so much, that in the space of six years, making an about face each year, he arrived to be marquis . . . of Villena, and lord of other great towns and places, and of many other inheritances and grants. . . . And equally by this path, against all justice, he had the mastership of Calatrava for his brother Pedro Girón.[13]

From 1440 almost to the end of the reign of Juan II there existed four distinct blocs: the king and Alvaro de Luna, Enrique and Juan Pacheco, the greater Castilian nobles, and the Infantes of Aragon. María, the queen, emerged as a leader in her own right and generally opposed the king, at times working with Enrique, and at other times with the Infantes. The political history of the period is largely the story of the shifting alliances and realignments among the four factions. The desirable goal was to be *à trois* in the political mixture, but more often the arrangement was two and two.

An assessment of the motives of the various groups and players is difficult, both because none left a clear statement of purpose and because the

12. Fernán Pérez de Guzmán, *La crónica del serenísimo príncipe Don Juan, segundo rey deste nombre en Castilla y en León*, ed. Cayetano Rosell, in *Biblioteca de autores españoles* 68 (Madrid, 1953), pp. 569, 574; Carrillo, *Crónica del halconero*, pp. 234–35, 308, 335–36, 340–46; Luis Suárez Fernández, "Los Trastámaras de Castilla y Aragón en el siglo XV (1407-74)," in vol. 15 of *Historia de España*, ed. Ramón Menéndez Pidal (Madrid, 1964), pp. 162–65; Jaime Vicens Vives, *Juan II de Aragón (1398-1479): Monarquía y revolución en la España del siglo XV* (Barcelona, 1953), pp. 82–83, 93–96.
13. Carrillo, *Crónica del halconero*, pp. 342–45.

actions of each are contradictory at times, but the attempt must be made to clarify the political narrative. The king, Juan II, presents the least difficulty. By all accounts he was far more satisfied in the role of patron of the arts than that of practical governor of the kingdom and gladly delegated the uninspiring task of administration to Alvaro de Luna. Luna proved himself a devoted servitor of Juan II but at the same time worked to extend his own territorial holdings and those of his family. Owing everything he had to Juan, Alvaro de Luna saw a strong monarchy as his best protection and constantly resisted any attempt to challenge the power of the king.

The Infantes of Aragon, in possession of vast Castilian territories, sought to maintain and enlarge their holdings. It was to their advantage to have Castile governed by a weak or ineffective monarch. Working constantly with forces from the Aragonese kingdom, the Infantes of Aragon were able at times to draw into their political and military maneuvers Castilian nobles who shared their common hatred of Alvaro de Luna or who saw an opportunity to extend their holdings through collaboration.

The most dangerous of the Infantes was the *segundón* (second son) Juan, who felt most keenly this later exclusion from Castile and who worked most strongly to assert his will there. Through marriage he controlled Navarre. Until he gained the crown of Aragon in 1458, the chronicles and documents refer to him as King Juan of Navarre, although he was never actually sovereign in that kingdom. When his elder brother Alfonso the Magnificent moved his center of operation to southern Italy, Juan became his lieutenant in the peninsular kingdoms and used this base to harass Castile tirelessly in an attempt to renew his influence there. Possibly because he recalled with distaste an early imprisonment in the Italian wars, Juan seems to have had an aversion to Italy, and never showed Naples and Sicily the interest his brother had.

The nobles of Castile differed so greatly in their outlook and so often changed their allegiances that it is nearly impossible to define their interests in a comprehensive fashion. Moved by pragmatic urges, individual *grandes* changed sides as they saw the political tides shift one way or another. They followed no consistent line in politics or ideology but generally were swayed by the exigencies of the moment.

The motivation of the prince of Asturias is the most difficult to analyze. Enrique apparently developed hostility toward his father, but the sparse documentation means that the scope and extent of his disaffection remain unanswered questions. The influence of his mother may have turned the son away from his father, but it is impossible to determine the ways in which María affected her son. The sources provide little illumination of such questions. The most compelling explanation of María's position is that she always felt more influenced by her heritage as one of the Infantes of Aragon than by affection and respect for her husband. Juan Pacheco's sway over Enrique is better documented; he consistently tried to dominate Enrique, both during Juan II's life and after Enrique became king. All through his career Pacheco's sole aim was to make himself the single most important power in the kingdom. He played on Enrique's reluctance to rule and generosity to build up vast holdings for himself and the members of his family. Enrique sporadically resisted Pacheco, but never effectively enough.

The first real break between Juan and Enrique occurred in 1441 when Juan and Alvaro prepared for war against the Infantes. Juan ordered Enrique to move on Guadalajara and take it. Enrique refused and remained in Madrid for a time before going to Segovia, always his favorite retreat, and declaring his political independence. During 1441 a league was formed among the Castilian nobles in opposition to Alvaro de Luna and his influence over the king. Enrique was invited to join but initially refused. An attempt to reconcile the differences between the prince and the king failed and Enrique then aligned with the nobles.[14]

In his first overt act against the interests of his father, in which the chronicler asserts he was influenced by his mother on the instructions of Juan of Navarre, Enrique in June 1441 attempted to take Tordesillas with six hundred foot soldiers and horsemen. Juan II heard of this and sent reinforcements under Pedro de Montealegre. Late one night Enrique arrived before the city gate and demanded admission. Montealegre replied, "Who is this who is calling?" "I am the prince, son of the king." Montealgre informed him, "Señor, I entered this town in the service of the king your father and on his mandate, and I do not think I should open to you at this hour unless you have a special authorization from my lord the king, your father." Without replying, Enrique turned back.[15]

Beginning in 1441 we find archival evidence that the prince was starting to make grants to nobles on his own authority. One of the first was to Iñigo López de Mendoza.[16] In 1441 or 1442 we find him giving Luis de

14. Pérez, *Crónica de Juan II*, pp. 574–75; Suárez, "Los Trastámaras," pp. 165–67; Vicens, *Juan II de Aragón*, pp. 100–101. These sources give 1441 as the beginning of the league, but in January 1440 the queen, her brothers Juan and Enrique, and many Castilian nobles signed a confederation: RAH, *Salazar*, *leg*. K-36, fols. 125–27v.

15. Pérez, *Crónica de Juan II*, p. 584.

16. AHN, *Osuna*, *leg*. 1827, fols. 9–15b.

Portocarrero 50,000 maravedís.[17] Enrique's first recorded grants to Pacheco came in 1442, with Pacheco receiving Campillo, Monasterio (unidentified), and Las Posas.[18]

In 1441 a league emerged with Enrique, his mother, and Fadrique Enríquez (the admiral of Castile) at its head, to whose actions Alvaro de Luna was forced to accede. In Burgos in September, the prince and the queen were able to deprive Luna of at least nine fortresses.[19]

Throughout 1442 and 1443 the power of the coalition of nobles and their Aragonese allies increased, and they were even able to imprison Juan II. This act caused Enrique to abandon his dealings with the league and compose his differences with his father. Breaking with the Infantes, María secured the release of Juan II. The king then reconfirmed Enrique's title as prince of Asturias, and the prince responded by instructing his followers to co-operate in the royal campaign Luna was waging against the league and the Aragonese, culminating in the first battle of Olmedo in May 1445. The royal forces, with the prince initiating the combat, were victorious and the Aragonese were driven from Castile.[20]

After Olmedo, with the Aragonese decisively expelled from Castile, the king and Alvaro de Luna moved to secure the position of the crown by punishing the rebels and rewarding the faithful with lands abandoned by the defeated. Alvaro de Luna received the title of count of Alburquerque and the towns of Trujillo, Medellín, and Cuéllar, lands which would fall to Beltrán de la Cueva when Enrique became king. Iñigo López de Mendoza added the marquisate of Santillana to his patrimony. Juan de Guzmán became the duke of Medina Sidonia. Enrique expanded his sizable holdings with the towns of Logroño, Ciudad Rodrigo, Jaén, and Cáceres, while Pacheco became marquis of Villena and his brother Pedro Girón master of Calatrava. Perhaps feeling that too general a weakening of the nobility might make Luna too great a threat, Enrique kept his father from severely

17. RAH, *Salazar*, *leg.* M-117, *hojas* 241–42.

18. Ibid., *leg.* M-9, fols. 406–406v; AHN, *Osuna*, *leg.* 3093, fol. 1.

19. RAH, *Salazar*, *leg.* M-10, fols. 29v, 239–51v. Luis Suárez Fernández, *Nobleza y monarquía: Puntos de vista sobre la historia castellana del siglo XV*, 2nd. ed. (Valladolid, 1975), p. 154.

20. Pérez, *Crónica de Juan II*, pp. 606–624, 626; Carrillo, *Crónica del halconero*, pp. 451, 454, 459, 463–65; Suárez, "Los Trastámaras," pp. 177–80, 183; Vicens, *Juan II de Aragón*, pp. 109–23; *Colección diplomática*, doc.7. Enrique and María were aided in their successful freeing of Juan II by a pact between Pedro and Alvaro de Stúñiga, father and son, and Pedro Fernández de Velasco and Pedro de Velasco, father and son, directed toward the same end: RAH, *Salazar*, *leg.* K-36, fols. 132–34.

punishing the most prominent of the defeated nobles, thereby preventing the settlement after Olmedo from being as conclusive as it might have been.[21]

In the same year, 1445, Pacheco and Enrique reorganized the resistance to Alvaro de Luna. Luna apparently recognized the danger and sought to counteract it by arranging a future marriage between the now widowed Juan II and Isabel of Portugal, daughter of the Portuguese regent Pedro, an agreement from which it was hoped Portuguese aid would flow. In Enrique's camp Pacheco was not inactive, and by the end of the year Enrique had achieved sufficient power to balance that of Alvaro de Luna.[22]

In the twelve months following Olmedo, Pacheco and Girón materially expanded their possessions by means of grants from the prince. Girón received the towns of Tiedra and Ureña, together with the *tercias* (part of the royal income) of Arévalo and the rights of income in various Andalusian towns.[23] Enrique awarded Pacheco a grant of one thousand vassals in the towns of Villena, Sax, Yecla, and some small places in the jurisdiction of Alarcón.[24]

The first months of the year 1446 saw the sides drawn for a full-scale war between the followers of Luna and the king against Enrique's faction, but the climax was avoided as both sides decided to negotiate. In the agreement of Astudillo (14 May 1446) what amounted to a division of government was worked out. Enrique vowed to respect the holdings of his father, but more importantly, Juan agreed to respect those of his son. They consented to a detailed distribution of the Castilian towns. Justice was made the joint responsibility of Luna and Pacheco.[25]

21. *Crónica de Alvaro de Luna*, pp. 155–57, 161–62; Pérez, *Crónica de Juan II*, pp. 626–28; Carrillo, *Crónica del halconero*, p. 466; Vicens, *Juan II de Aragón*, p. 126. Juan's grant of the marquisate of Santillana to Iñigo López de Mendoza and later confirmations, AHN, *Osuna*, *leg*. 1784, fols. 1, 2–6; *leg*. 1790, fols. 1–2. For Medina Sidonia's grants, Ladero Quesada, *Andalucía en el siglo XV*, p. 5. Shortly after Olmedo Fadrique Enríquez was outlawed, and within a month Enrique was negotiating with him with offers of restitution: RAH, *Salazar*, *leg*. M-58, fol. 106.
22. Pérez, *Crónica de Juan II*, pp. 630–31, 633–34; Suárez, "Los Trastámaras," pp. 187–88. Alonso de Palencia, *Crónica de Enrique IV*, trans. Antonio Paz y Meliá, 2 vols., in *Biblioteca de autores españoles* 207–208 (Madrid, 1973-75), 1:28–29, accused Luna of having poisoned Juan II's first wife María.
23. AHN, *Osuna*, *caja* 2, nos. 3–5; *leg*. 35, fol. 46. *Tercias* were 2/9 of the church's tithe on agricultural products, regularly ceded to the crown. Miguel Angel Ladero Quesada, *La hacienda real de Castilla en el siglo XV* (La Laguna, 1973), p. 39.
24. RAH, *Salazar*, *leg*. D-14, fols. 128–31; *leg*. M-90, fols. 101–101v.
25. Pérez, *Crónica de Juan II*, pp. 641–50; Carrillo, *Crónica del halconero*, pp. 470–71; Suárez, "Los Trastámaras," pp. 190–91; Vicens, *Juan II de Aragón*, pp. 128–29. Madrigal is the place given according to RAH, *Salazar*, *leg*. K-2, fols. 418–29v.

A confused period ensued during 1447 and 1448. Neither side paid much attention to the agreement. Luna and Juan tried to purchase support from the great nobles. Aware of the unrest, the Aragonese king, Alfonso V, began new moves against Castile. The previous year he had attempted to get Pope Eugenius IV to use the powers of the papal office to revoke Alvaro de Luna's election as master of Santiago. The Granadans added to the general ferment by beginning a campaign of territorial enlargement. As the culmination of a lengthy Aragonese diplomatic maneuver, Juan II pardoned the admiral Fadrique Enríquez and allowed the marriage of his daughter Juana to the widowed Juan of Navarre.[26]

After his marriage with Isabel of Portugal in 1447, Juan II of Castile almost immediately began to turn against Alvaro de Luna. The new queen's hostility was an unforeseen blow to Luna. The marriage itself was part of the major shift in foreign policy engineered by Luna. In the new diplomacy Portugal was to replace Aragon as the keystone of Castilian relations; it was a policy continued by Enrique IV. By a very interesting political maneuver in 1448, Luna and Pacheco tried to reach a personal agreement to run the country, believing they had full control over their nominal lords. The logical move for the king and prince would have been to turn against their favorites and work together, but neither trusted the other.[27] Any hope of accommodation between father and son was ended in 1449 by the imbroglio over Toledo.

Previously, in 1445, Juan had placed a new lieutenant in Toledo, Pedro Sarmiento, a move which had extremely complicated repercussions. Enrique at the time objected because he felt this would increase Luna's power.[28] After several years Sarmiento began working with the Aragonese. Actually he was attempting to make himself independent in Toledo, and his activities soon assumed the proportions of an actual revolt. His tactics included seizure of property and real estate, suspension of laws, imprisonments, torture and killings of his rivals, and the fomenting of anti-Semitism. More ominously, he issued a *Sententia-estatuto* which supposedly restated earlier Castilian laws denying public office to any converted Jew.[29] In fact, it extended anti-Jewish legislation to *conversos*. Sarmiento tried to justify his revolt as an expression of the rights of the city in popular protest

26. Pérez, *Crónica de Juan II*, pp. 652, 654; Suárez, "Los Trastámaras," p. 194; Vicens, *Juan II de Aragón*, pp. 127, 129, 131. Enríquez was still exiled.
27. Pérez, *Crónica de Juan II*, pp. 656–58.
28. Suárez, "Los Trastámaras," pp. 189–90.
29. Eloy Benito Ruano, *Toledo en el siglo XV: Vida política* (Madrid, 1961), pp. 38–39, 44, 47–49.

against Alvaro de Luna.[30] When Juan sought admission to the city he was greeted by bombardments and the shouted taunts of Sarmiento's adherents as each shot cleared the walls:

> Toma allá esa naranja
> Que te embian desde la granja.[31]

Perhaps because he realized he could not resist the royal forces for very long, Sarmiento tried to induce Enrique to join him. In March 1449 Alvaro de Luna persuaded Enrique not to deal with the rebels, but in June, breaking the agreement, Enrique arranged to divide the control of Toledo with Sarmiento. In July the fever aroused by Sarmiento broke out with a sacking of the Jewish quarter. Shortly after this Enrique entered the city and was mistakenly hailed as a deliverer by the revolt's victims. However, he could do little more than garrison a few key points and retire. He was scheduled to return in November, and at that time he broke his journey to engage in a boar hunt near Toledo. For perhaps the only time in his life Enrique gained a decisive political advantage from his love of the chase. During the delay a follower of Sarmiento received a fatal wound in a bullfight in Toledo. On his deathbed he revealed to his confessor the existence of a plot by Sarmiento against the prince. The priest sent word to Enrique. Forewarned, Enrique entered the city fully prepared, ejected Sarmiento, and assumed full control of Toledo.[32]

During this same time, the spring and early summer of 1449, another league of nobles began to challenge the power of Juan and Alvaro de Luna. This particularly powerful league was directed by Pacheco. Juan of Navarre also sent troops. Just on the verge of what appeared to be a decisive victory of the faction opposed to the king, Enrique backed down and entered into an agreement with his father. This seriously damaged the carefully conceived plans of Pacheco and is a clear refutation of the recurring charge that Enrique was only a tool of his favorites. For over two years after this Enrique and Pacheco were estranged. Even so, as Suárez Fernández states, after 1449 Enrique was the most powerful figure in the kingdom.[33]

Despite this the prince failed to follow up his advantages; he may then have realized the precarious situation of his father's government and have recognized the need to preserve it. In 1451 at the Cortes of Valladolid and

30. Ibid., p. 38.
31. "Take this orange sent to you from the garden!" Pérez, *Crónica de Juan II*, p. 664.
32. Benito Ruano, *Toledo*, pp. 44–58.
33. Suárez, "Los Trastámaras," pp. 201–204.

in a private meeting at Tordesillas, he patched up all remaining differences with his father and Alvaro de Luna. He even agreed to participate in an expedition to Navarre with his father.[34]

In 1452 Enrique abruptly withdrew from active political participation. At just this point the sources fail and we are forced to piece together a very incomplete picture. Alfonso the Magnificent may have offered aid to overthrow Luna and give the government to Enrique in return for the restitution of the Castilian holdings of the Infantes and their followers, but nothing matured.[35] Luna apparently still had a residue of influence over the king, but royal power was weakened. Juan was reduced to government by persuasion. Finally, in late 1452 or early 1453 the king, influenced by his wife, as all the sources insist, decided to overthrow Luna. Pacheco and Girón may even have offered to help Luna, but he refused. As Juan acted and had Luna beheaded in Valladolid in June 1453, Enrique did not choose to assert his power. He continued to shun political activity for the last year before his father's death on 21 July 1454.[36]

Legal proceedings also kept the prince occupied. On 27 July 1453, just a year before his father's death, Enrique secured a divorce from Blanca de Navarra after years of childless marriage.

An additional explanation for Enrique's political inactivity is found in the chronicle of Pérez de Guzmán. Commenting on the king's death, the chronicler reported:

> It is certain that [the king] had determined to leave the kingdom to the Infante don Alfonso his son, but he had to consider that because of the great power that prince [Enrique] had, there would be great agitation in the kingdoms.[37]

It is very difficult to interpret this evidence. The chronicle itself was not put into final form until the reign of Carlos I (1516-1555) and it underwent revision during the reign of the *Reyes Católicos.* It is possible that the passage was inserted then to discredit Enrique. But if it is accurate it could explain Enrique's inactivity in the last years of Juan's reign. Many of the prince's followers were enemies of Luna and no doubt urged him to

34. Ibid., pp. 205–206; *Crónica de Alvaro de Luna*, pp. 265–68. Enrique returned Toledo to the king.
35. Vicens, *Juan II de Aragón*, pp. 152–54.
36. Suárez, "Los Trastámaras," pp. 208–213; J.F. O'Callaghan, "Don Pedro Girón: Master of the Order of Calatrava," *Hispania* 21 (1961):364; *Colección diplomática*, docs. 20–29, 38. Juan's embargo on Luna's property: RAH, *Salazar*, *leg*. F-41, fols. 112–18.
37. Pérez, *Crónica de Juan II*, p. 692.

oppose the favorite actively. But if Enrique had combined forces with the king, the victorious Juan might have suborned many of his son's followers and the power the prince possessed might have evaporated. Also, if the queen could engineer the ouster and execution of Alvaro de Luna, perhaps she could have persuaded Juan to settle the kingdom on her own son Alfonso (born 15 November 1453)[38] at the expense of her stepson Enrique. The chronicle seems to indicate this. If such a maneuver were in progress and Enrique knew of it, all the more reason for him to remain aloof and maintain his forces. Even though the threat of a successful maneuver using the newly born Alfonso as a figurehead was slight, Enrique could not discount the legal and political difficulties a disputed succession would cause him.

From this examination of his principate we can see the beginnings of the problems of Enrique's reign—both the problems he faced and the problems that his historian faces. Most obviously, the legacy of endemic factional struggles and civil wars of his father's reign made it impossible for Enrique's rule to be anything but stormy. That he nonetheless imposed a considerable degree of stability for the first ten years of his reign was a tremendous accomplishment.

One of the most serious accusations made against Enrique as king is that he had no will of his own and was merely the creature of his advisers. Based on the evidence of his activity as prince of Asturias, we must modify that judgment. Undoubtedly Pacheco did exert a great influence over the young prince, but Enrique could refuse to comply with Pacheco's wishes in decisive matters and at moments of critical importance. Later, Enrique would surround himself with more than one adviser, and at no time did any favorite—not even Pacheco or Beltrán de la Cueva—occupy a position analogous to that of Alvaro de Luna in Juan's reign.

As king, Enrique pursued consistent, rational, and intelligent policies in internal political affairs, as well as in diplomacy and economics. His years as prince of Asturias do not give us much basis for drawing conclusions in those areas. He was, for most of the period, acquiring a political education. He did not have the time or opportunity to demonstrate what he had learned before he reached the throne.

38. Juan Torres Fontes, *El príncipe Don Alfonso, 1465-1468* (Murcia, 1971), pp. 99, 141–42.

IV

KING OF CASTILE

In a simple ceremony customary since the fourteenth century, Enrique IV took the crown of Castile on 23 July 1454 in Valladolid. Juan II had definitely declared him his legal heir, and there were no reservations as to his right to the throne. Physically he was handsome except for a broken nose, the result of a childhood accident. He was blond and blue-eyed with long hair and a beard, and his contemporaries considered him a tall man. In all his dealings with his subjects, the chroniclers tell us, he showed a welcome lack of ceremony; he disliked having his hands kissed as a sign of respect and refused to address his inferiors with the slightly contemptuous familiar *tu*. Uncomfortable in large gatherings, Enrique preferred to associate with smaller groups. In fact, ruling and the trappings of monarchy bored him; he much preferred hunting or quiet contemplation on walks through the forest. Though not indolent, he was an energetic ruler only when forced to be, and he was a poor judge of men. Yet these flaws would not have doomed his reign to failure; the complexity of events did that.[1]

At the beginning of that reign, however, success seemed not only possible but likely. We must not let knowledge of the end of Enrique's twenty-year rule influence our estimation of its beginnings. For nearly the entire first decade, Enrique was an effective ruler, authoritative in his actions. During the whole reign he undertook a series of reforms which his successors would continue. An examination of his policies and innovations, especially

1. Juan II's will and its codicil, giving Enrique full rights of succession, are in *Colección diplomática*, docs. 46–47. Diego de Valera, *Memorial de diversas hazañas*, ed. Juan de Mata Carriazo, Colección de crónicas españoles, no. 4 (Madrid, 1941), p. 4; Diego Enríquez del Castillo, *Crónica del rey Don Enrique el cuarto de este nombre*, ed. Cayetano Rosell, in vol. 70 of *Biblioteca de autores españoles* (Madrid, 1953), pp. 100–101. Fernando del Pulgar, *Claros varones de Castilla*, ed. R.B. Tate (Oxford, 1971), p. 5. The consistently hostile Alonso de Palencia tried to assert that Enrique was not the legitimate heir, but all other sources disagree. Palencia, *Crónica de Enrique IV*, trans. Antonio Paz y Meliá, 2 vols., in *Biblioteca de autores españoles* 207–208 (Madrid, 1973-75), 1:9. Palencia (*Crónica*, 1:11) also described Enrique as having a face like a monkey—due to a broken nose—but with handsome hair and a well formed body and limbs.

those made in the first ten years, offers significant points for a rehabilitation of Enrique IV.

Enrique began his reign a rich man. Since there was no new heir apparent, he kept the lands and incomes of the prince of Asturias in addition to his personal possessions. To this he added the regal holdings, which recently had been swelled by the confiscation of Alvaro de Luna's property. But if he had material wealth, his familial legacy was one of poverty. From his father he had learned nothing to help him to be an assertive ruler; Juan II's cardinal rule of political activity had been delegation. His mother had apparently been an energetic and resourceful woman who shared the legacy of political skills of the Infantes of Aragon, but she had been dead for some ten years, and even before her death her relations with her son are hard to determine, although their names did appear together at the head of various political alliances. Enrique had no support from siblings; his half sister and brother Isabel and Alfonso were still very young. His closest adult relatives were his uncles—the old Infantes of Aragon. Alfonso V (who was to die in 1458) had for years abandoned peninsular affairs to concentrate on his Italian ventures from his residence in Naples, and Juan (Alfonso's successor in Aragon) was to prove Enrique's most tenacious enemy. His queen gave only sporadic assistance.[2] So it is not surprising that Enrique sought aid and advice from a series of favorites. That he was unable to find loyal and consistent supporters was a large part of his tragedy.

Seeking peace within his kingdom, Enrique organized his government on conciliatory lines. Many of the councillors and officials of his father's reign stayed in their places. In the appointment records 159 individuals appear who retained their offices from Juan's reign into Enrique's.[3] Those imprisoned or exiled in the previous reign were pardoned. He released Diego Manrique and Fernán Alvarez de Toledo and allowed the admiral Fadrique Enríquez to return to his lands, which were returned to him after having been impounded. He pardoned Juan de Luna and gave a general pardon to Pedro Fajardo. The king sought through these concessions to win widespread adherence to his government and avoid the formation of noble plots directed against him.[4]

2. Part of this has been suggested by Antonio Bermejo de la Rica, *El triste destino de Enrique IV y La Beltraneja* (Madrid, n.d. [1945]), pp. 149–50.

3. AGS, *Quitaciones de Corte*, *legs*. 1–4.

4. Enríquez, *Crónica*, pp. 102–103. Documents restoring the admiral's property are in AHN, *Osuna*, *leg*. 496, fol. 4, and *carpeta* 62, no. 8. Juan de Luna's pardon, AHN, *Osuna*, *leg*. 2244, fol. 2. Fajardo's pardon is cited in Juan Torres Fontes, *Itinerario de Enrique IV de Castilla* (Murcia, 1955), p. 38.

When Enrique took the throne, he embarked immediately on a policy designed to forge alliances with members of the nobility to secure his power, offering grants in return for loyalty. He made the marshall Diego Fernández de Córdoba count of Cabra in 1455. The Córdobas had been lords of Aguilar and held lands in the modern provinces of Córdoba and Jaén. He favored the Extremaduran family of Figueroa with the title of count of Feria and the governorship of Extremadura. In 1455 he created Pedro Portocarrero as count of Medellín. In the same year Juan de Silva became count of Cifuentes and Lope Sánchez de Moscoso count of Altamira.[5] The next year Pedro Alvarez Osorio became count of Lemos.[6] But Enrique's early grants were not confined to new entrants to the titled ranks; the already powerful got favors too. Pedro de Acuña became the chief officer of the Mesta.[7] The Stúñiga family received early concessions: Alvaro de Stúñiga, already count of Plasencia, gained monetary and territorial gifts;[8] Diego López de Stúñiga became count of Miranda in 1457;[9] and in 1455 Pedro de Stúñiga was named chief customs official.[10] Juan Ponce de León, count of Arcos, received a monetary grant.[11] Although relations between Enrique and the Mendoza family were somewhat strained early in his reign, he did confirm the privileges of Lorenzo Suárez de Figueroa, a younger son of the old marquis of Santillana.[12]

Enrique's policy of creating new *grandes* from the lower ranks of the nobility in an effort to dilute the power of the aristocracy and create allies can best be seen in his favor for four men: Juan Pacheco and his brother Pedro Girón, Miguel Lucas de Iranzo, and Beltrán de la Cueva, the first two before he became king, the others after. In the political strife of

5. Lowell W. Newton, "The Development of the Castilian Peerage" (unpublished Ph. D. dissertation, Tulane University, 1972), pp. 240–41, has a list of the titles granted by Enrique IV. For Juan de Silva, see RAH, *Salazar*, *leg*. M-94, *hojas* 263–80v. For Diego Fernández de Córdoba, see Miguel Angel Ladero Quesada, *Andalucía en el siglo XV: Estudios de historia política* (Madrid, 1973), p. 111.
6. Seville, 26 June 1456, cited in Torres Fontes, *Itinerario*, p. 59.
7. RAH, *Salazar*, *leg*. D-13, fols. 86–89; *leg*. M-5, fol. 272; *leg*. M-27, fols. 251v–53.
8. Grant of the villa of Pesquera, AHN, *Osuna*, *caja* 6, no. 4; of Gibraleón (which he received jointly with his wife), ibid., *caja* 6, no. 14; of Curiel, ibid., *caja* 11, no. 2; of Grañón, ibid., *leg*. 321, fol. 3; of the *alcabalas* of Roa, ibid., *leg*. 306, fol. 3; of Burquillos and the surrounding area, ibid., *leg*. 339, no. 9; of Stúñiga's right to found a *mayorazgo*, ibid., *leg*. 214, fol. 20.
9. Cited in Torres Fontes, *Itinerario*, p. 70.
10. RAH, *Salazar*, *leg*. M-59, fol. 60v–62.
11. AHN, *Osuna*, *carpeta* 3, no. 6.
12. RAH, *Salazar*, *leg*. O-20, fols. 44–64v. He also secured the homage of Seville's most prominent nobles, Juan de Guzmán and Juan Ponce de León, although it took two years to achieve: AHN, *Osuna*, *leg*. 1635, fols. 3–10.

Enrique's reign, the most highly visible was Juan Pacheco, who became a favored servitor of the future king while Enrique was prince of Asturias. An extremely able politician, Pacheco received the title of marquis of Villena as a result of his aid to Juan II in the first battle of Olmedo. At the same time his brother Pedro Girón received the mastership of the military order of Calatrava, and from that privileged position he built a huge collection of estates for his posterity. The lands of the marquesado of Villena occupied a vital expanse of territory on the eastern frontier of Castile to the north of Murcia. It covered important trading networks and encompassed pastures, vineyards, and truck gardens. After Enrique's succession, Pacheco steadily increased his holdings and titles. In the first year of the new reign he was named a *guarda mayor* and in 1458 marshall of Castile. Through the vicissitudes of the involuted political manuevers, Pacheco steadily advanced himself. In 1460 he got the countship of Xiquena. Later he was one of the leaders of the unsuccessful revolt against the king, but thereafter he return to royal favor.[13]

Miguel Lucas de Iranzo, from a lower noble background, was one of the key figures early in Enrique's reign. Created count of Quesada in 1458, he received appointments as *alcaide*, *falconero mayor*, constable, and chief chancellor of the royal seal. But in somewhat mysterious circumstances, probably due to a quarrel with Pacheco's faction, he left the royal court and devoted himself to activity in and near Jaén.[14]

Beltrán de la Cueva, whose father Diego was a councilman in Ubeda, advanced steadily in Enrique's service, despite the growing opposition of Pacheco. He became a *guarda* in 1456 and two years later was named *mayordomo mayor* and *maestresala.* In 1462 he became count of Ledesma. As a sign of his support, Enrique appointed him master of Santiago in 1464.

13. For Pacheco's royal offices, AGS, *Quitaciones de Corte*, *leg*. 3. Girón received the right to found a *mayorazgo* (AHN, *Osuna*, *leg*. 1, fol. 15), and in 1454 Enrique confirmed his possessions: tax rights in Jaén, Fuesada, Ubeda, Baeza, and Andújar (ibid., *carpeta* 1, no. 14); in Arévalo and Peñafiel (ibid., *carpeta* 9, fol. 10); and the towns of Ureña, Tiedra, San Felices de los Gallegos (ibid., *leg*. 105, fol. 4). Pacheco had all his rights confirmed during the Cortes of Córdoba, 6 June 1455, RAH, *Salazar*, *leg*. O–20, fol. 119. Specific confirmations included his right to found a *mayorazgo* (22 August 1455, ibid., *leg*. O–20 fol. 119v) and his possession of Jumilla (AHN, *Osuna*, *códices*, 1022B). In 1456 Enrique legitimized two of Pacheco's children, Juan Pacheco and Isabel de Menenses, RAH, *Salazar*, *leg*. D-14, fols. 26–27, and *leg*. M-45, fols. 266–70.

14. AGS, *Quitaciones de Corte*, *leg*. 4; *Hechos del Condestable Don Miguel Lucas de Iranzo*, ed. Juan de Mata Carriazo, Colección de crónicas españoles, no. 3 (Madrid, 1941). The patent of nobility granted to Lucas is printed in *Colección diplomática*, doc. 49.

Pacheco, who had wanted Santiago for himself, helped to launch the revolt against the crown. Enrique gave in to the aristocrats' demand that Beltrán be stripped of the mastership but compensated him generously with the towns of Roa, Aranda, Molina, Atienza, and Cuéllar in addition to the title of duke of Alburquerque. In the last year of Enrique's reign he was also named count of Huelma. His lands along the Portuguese border encouraged him to support Enrique's diplomatic approaches to that kingdom.[15]

But lands, titles, and royal offices were not the only way Enrique rewarded his followers. Monetary grants to favored supporters were often lavish. Those of Beltrán de la Cueva, while among the most munificent, serve to illustrate the general course. In the period from 1460 to 1465, he received a total of over three and one-half million maravedís in grants of various kinds,[16] and this was at a time when a royal clerk (*escribano de cámara*) received a yearly salary of 8,400 maravedís and the most highly paid judicial officials (*oidores de la Audiencia*) received 40,000 maravedís per annum.[17]

Throughout his reign Enrique pursued policies designed to improve the kingdom and increase royal control; in many respects Fernando and Isabel continued in the path Enrique marked. His most obvious anticipation was in his appointment practices for royal officials. A general fashion among western European monarchies in the period of transition from medieval to modern times was the introduction of increasing numbers of university graduates (known as *letrados* in Castile) into administrative positions. The university-trained officials were not necessarily more highly educated (as opposed to those trained by apprenticeship) or better suited for office, but the kings clearly preferred them, not the least because they could be counted on to offer the monarchs greater personal loyalty. One of the older assumptions about the growth of royal service in Castile is that Fernando and Isabel swept the payroll of nobles and replaced them with *letrados*. From my study of the apointment records at the archive of Simancas, this impression clearly should be revised.[18] In both aristocratic and university-educated royal officials, there was a clear progression throughout the fifteenth century.

15. AGS, *Quitaciones de Corte*, *leg*. 2; Antonio Rodríguez Villa, *Bosquejo biográfico de Don Beltrán de la Cueva* (Madrid, 1881); Ladero Quesada, *Andalucía en el siglo XV*, p. 62.
16. AGS, *Mercedes y privilegios*, *leg*. 1, fol. 682; *leg*. 52, fol. 3.
17. AGS, *Quitaciones de Corte, legs*. 2–4.
18. The statistics which follow are taken from three sections in AGS: *Quitaciones de Corte, Nóminas de Corte, Casa y Sitios Reales.* A cautionary note is in order. It is

APPOINTMENTS: ROYAL OFFICIALS

	Reign of Juan II (1406-54)	Reign of Enrique IV (1454-74)	Reign of Fernando and Isabel (1474-1516)
Aristocrats	16	33	53
Bachilleres	11	44	18
Licenciados	6	32	73
Doctores	17	21	46
All *letrados*	34	97	137

From this we can clearly see that nothing changed radically when Fernando and Isabel became rulers. They simply followed the existing pattern set by Juan II and expanded by Enrique IV.

The figures become even more meaningful when they are examined within occupational categories. Various types of *abogados* (lawyers), *oidores* and *jueces* (both meaning judges), and *alcaldes* make up the judicial and legal category. *Alcaldes* are placed here; they had both judicial and executive functions, but in the fifteenth century the judicial was predominant.

APPOINTMENTS: LEGAL AND JUDICIAL

	Reign of Juan II	Reign of Enrique IV	Reign of Fernando and Isabel
Total number of appointments	54	124	79
Number with academic titles	22	74	46
Percentage with academic titles	40.7%	59%	58.2%
Number with noble titles	4	3	0
Percentage with noble titles	7.4%	2.4%	0

impossible to determine how closely the number of preserved documents corresponds to the actual number issued. I have checked the higher officials in the archival sources against the chronicles and found a fairly close correspondence. So while the figures are not absolute, they are indicative. An extended study of this material will soon appear in *Societas: A Review of Social History.*

In this category there was a clear trend away from employment of nobles and toward use of *letrados*. This tendency was well established by Enrique IV's reign and changed little by the time of Fernando and Isabel.

In the medical category there were no nobles, since surgery and medicine traditionally had been shunned by the European nobility. The *boticarios* (pharmacists), *cirujanos* (surgeons), *físicos* and *médicos* (physicians) could hold either academic or non-academic titles. Those in the second group were referred to as *maestres* and rabbis.

APPOINTMENTS: MEDICAL

	Reign of Juan II	Reign of Enrique IV	Reign of Fernando and Isabel
Total number of appointments	14	10	33
Number with academic titles	2	5	17
Percentage with academic titles	15%	50%	51.5%
Number with non-academic titles	2	2	4
Percentage with non-academic titles	15%	20%	12.1%

The level of educational status in the medical category clearly increased in the reign of Enrique IV and remained nearly constant under his successors.

I have grouped executive and military officials in a separate category. Included here are *alcaides*, *alguaciles*, *gobernadores*, and *corregidores*.

APPOINTMENTS: EXECUTIVE AND MILITARY

	Reign of Juan II	Reign of Enrique IV	Reign of Fernando and Isabel
Total number of appointments	247	200	143
Number with academic titles	0	0	28
Percentage with academic titles	0	0	19.6%
Total with noble titles	4	14	14
Percentage with noble titles	1.6%	7%	9.8%

We can see that the number and percentage of nobles in this grouping jumped in the reign of Enrique IV and held more or less steady in the reign of his successors. Academic titleholders do not make their appearance until the reign of Fernando and Isabel. There may be some significance here for the unjustified representation of the *Reyes Católicos* as the great innovators in the employment of *letrados*. The appointees in this category were no doubt the most visible, both in the period and in the period's chronicles, and this may have led earlier historians—relying heavily on the chroniclers—to erroneous conclusions.

Fiscal, secretarial, and conciliar officials, together with household staff and confessors, make up the administrative and household category.

APPOINTMENTS: ADMINISTRATIVE AND HOUSEHOLD

	Reign of Juan II	Reign of Enrique IV	Reign of Fernando and Isabel
Total number of appointments	157	287	299
Number with academic titles	5	13	59
Percentage with academic titles	3.2%	4.5%	19.7%
Number with noble titles	6	13	29
Percentage with noble titles	3.8%	4.5%	9.7%

In this category the number of university-educated officials makes its greatest leap in the reign of the *Reyes Católicos*, and there is also a leap (albeit smaller) in the number of nobles they employed.

From these figures it is apparent that Fernando and Isabel continued to employ nobles and even increased their use. The trend toward the use of *letrados* in royal service was already firmly grounded by the reign of Enrique IV. This is a clear indication of the continuity which spanned the reign of Enrique and his successors.

In an effort to strengthen royal power, Enrique extended the already established practice of sending court-appointed officials into the municipalities to ensure that local practice conformed to the king's decrees and desires. As early as 1455, when he held his first Cortes, the representatives asked him not to send out *corregidores* (a fourteenth-century innovation) except when asked for locally. The *corregidores* were royal officials charged to sit on town councils and protect crown interests. Their use was one of the most successful means Fernando and Isabel had for asserting central authority, and clearly from the beginning of his reign Enrique was anticipating his successors. He also placed other officials in the town councils, appointed governors of fortresses and magistrates, and designated whom certain towns should elect as representatives to the Cortes. His methods must have been effective, since by 1462 the Cortes complained about the growing strength of royal officials and their proliferation, and earnestly requested that the centrally appointed officials be excluded from deliberations in the urban councils. Clearly Enrique's attempt at control from the center was effective enough to bring forth protests and gives an impression that contrasts sharply with his usual image as a bungler.[19]

With the significant exception of the kingdom of Aragon, the roots of the European diplomacy of Fernando and Isabel can be clearly seen in the reign of Enrique. Throughout his reign his chief difficulties came from the relentless opposition of Juan II of Aragon, who worked successfully to implant his influence in Castile, a policy spectacularly achieved through the marriage of his son Fernando with Isabel. And while he was doing so, Juan of Aragon schemed with dissident Castilian nobles and the Muslims of Granada to thwart Enrique's every move. As soon as their hold on Castile and Aragon was secure, the *Reyes Católicos* adopted Enrique's diplomatic orientation almost intact.

Portugal was clearly important for the neighboring kingdom. Enrique married the Portuguese princess Juana in 1454, and throughout his life he forged strong ties with the Portuguese royal house. Castilian-Portuguese relations degenerated into open war from 1474 to 1479, when Afonso V of Portugal espoused the daughter of Enrique IV and the cause of her succession. But after the end of the war, the traditional friendship between the two kingdoms returned and Fernando and Isabel sealed the alliance with royal marriages.

With the other kingdoms of western Europe, Enrique's diplomacy clearly anticipated that of his successors: trade with Flanders, overtures to England, and hostility toward France. Castile's economy was oriented toward the export of raw materials in return for manufactured goods. Castilian wool from the vast herds of Merino sheep fed the looms of the Low Countries, and leather, olive oil, fruit, and iron went there and to France and England. The regular Flemish trade was a constant feature of Castile's economy. From the middle of the fourteenth century, there had been close ties between France and Castile, allied in the Hundred Years' War. At the same time Anglo-Castilian relations naturally suffered checks

19. *Cortes*, vol. 3, Córdoba 1455: article 3, pp. 677–78, article 15, p. 689; Toledo 1462: article 1, pp. 704–705, article 6, p. 707, article 19, pp. 714–15, article 33, pp. 726–27, article 40, pp. 731–32, article 52, pp. 740–41. Document citations of Enrique's use of *corregidores* are found in Torres Fontes, *Itinerario*, pp. 70, 128, 145, 183. For other examples of royal interference in local government, ibid., pp. 36, 40, 129, 184.

as both sides raided the other's shipping. It is interesting to note that the northern Castilian towns customarily traded with England in contravention of normal royal policy. Acting almost in a sovereign manner, the league of Castilian coastal towns signed treaties with English monarchs in 1351 and 1474. Enrique IV, after an unsuccessful interview with Louis XI in 1463, altered his foreign policy and broke relations with France. By 1467 a treaty of commerce and friendship with England had replaced the traditional ties with France. Due to the pressure of his own subjects and the requests of the French, Enrique revoked the English alliance in 1471 but maintained ties of friendship until the end of his reign.[20] The increasing coolness of Franco-Castilian relations was the first anticipation of the diplomatic revolution which from the reign of Fernando and Isabel would find France and Spain opposed as hostile neighbors for the next two centuries. Historians have generally ascribed the ties of the united Spain with England and Flanders, sealed by royal marriages, to the anti-French legacy of the crown of Aragon, threatened as it was on its Pyrenean frontier and in its Italian designs, but we must note that this alliance system, so fundamental to the diplomacy of early modern Europe, also had a Castilian facet. Even before the Union of Crowns, Castile was moving toward hostility to France.

Enrique's policy toward the Islamic kingdom of Granada can be compared favorably to the very different campaign of the *Reyes Católicos.* In the fifteenth century, Granada covered a rough crescent in the south of the peninsula with strong-points at Gibraltar, Málaga, and the city of Granada. Far from constituting a danger for Castile, Granada served as a link between the Islamic and Christian worlds and routinely swelled the Castilian treasury with tribute money. As events showed, conquest of the mountainous territory would be extremely difficult and costly in men and money, so Enrique developed strategy and tactics which would bring maximum benefits from a minimum of cost and effort.[21] In his four campaigns in

20. See the request of the Cortes at Ocaña in 1469, *Cortes*, vol. 3, article 29, pp. 809–811. For reports that the French wished to resume the Castilian trade, see Enríquez, *Crónica*, pp. 184–85. Eleanora Mary Carus-Wilson, *Medieval Merchant Venturers*, 2nd. ed. (London, 1967), pp. 56–57; Luciano Serrano, *Los Reyes Católicos y la ciudad de Burgos, desde 1451 a 1492* (Madrid, 1943), p. 18; José Angel García de Cortázar, *Vizcaya en el siglo XV: Aspectos sociales y económicos* (Bilbao, 1966), pp. 180, 189, 233–37.

21. Miguel Angel Ladero Quesada, *Granada: Historia de un país islámico (1232-1571)* (Madrid, 1967), pp. 110–18. In another work Ladero Quesada put the verified expenses of the conquest down to 1492 at 600,000,000 maravedís, and he estimated the actual total to have been about 800,000,000 maravedís: *Castilla y la conquista del reino de Granada* (Valladolid, 1967), p. 202.

the years 1455 to 1458, he carried out his plans. Castilian forces were kept under firm control and used in short, rapid attacks on vulnerable points. Lengthy sieges at fortified locations were avoided, and the destruction of crops (although Enrique forbade the cutting of trees) added an economic weapon which heightened tensions in the Islamic kingdom. Conquest of fortresses had a low priority since Enrique felt that possession of new positions would give the Castilian nobles undue power, and that in Christian hands the fortresses would be a provocation for Muslim revenge. Enrique placed great emphasis on diplomacy: he dealt with dissident Muslim leaders to encourage them to work against the king of Granada, and the treaties he signed brought benefits to Castile in the form of additional tribute and repatriated Castilian warriors. Enrique's outlook is best indicated in a quotation from his court chronicler explaining the king's refusal to allow skirmishing.

> Because he was pious and not cruel, more a friend of the life of his [followers] than the spiller of their blood, he said that . . . the life of men had no price or equivalence, and it was a great error to risk them, and because of this it did not please him that his [followers] went out on skirmishes. . . . And in such expeditions, [too] much money was spent; he wished . . . [rather] to expend his treasures [in] damaging the enemies little by little. . . .[22]

Contrary to contemporary opinion, Enrique's Granadan policy was in many ways a great success. By the end of the first ten years of his reign, Castilian forces had secured important strategic positions such as Archidona and Gibraltar. Granada's economic and political position was weaker. The frontier was more secure than at the time of Enrique's succession, and the Castilians had clearly seized the military initiative.[23] In their decision to wage a conclusive campaign against the Muslims, the *Reyes Católicos* rejected Enrique's wiser policy of limited engagements and slow expansion. Their conquest, spectacular as it was, took over a decade and required vast expenditures of men and money, both of which had to be extracted from the kingdom. And in return for aristocratic support, they had to grant extensive concessions. Finally, the need for vast sums of money led them

22. Enríquez, *Crónica*, pp. 106–107; the quotation is on p. 107. Pulgar, *Claros varones*, p. 9; Juan Torres Fontes, "Las treguas con Granada de 1462 y 1463," *Hispania* 23 (1963):163–99; Juan Torres Fontes, *El príncipe Don Alfonso, 1465-1468* (Murcia, 1971), pp. 25–29.

23. Luis Suárez Fernández, *Juan II y la frontera de Granada* (Valladolid, 1954), p. 33.

to an increased use of deficit financing, a policy which would bankrupt Spain in the late sixteenth century.[24]

Enrique's success against Granada might have been greater if he had been able to pursue his strategy consistently, but in the latter years of his reign, noble revolts and Aragonese concerns prevented him from devoting more of his attention and the kingdom's resources to the southern campaigns. From the very beginning there were problems with his own nobles and clergy. The nobles did not agree with the limited war the king pursued. Together with their younger sons, they were out for glory and territorial possessions, and both were denied them in sufficient measure. Many of the clergy, imbued with the increasing spirit of religious intolerance, could not countenance any dealing with non-Christians that did not include conquest and conversion. From such attitudes would later come the accusations that the king was lax or even hostile toward Christianity—accusations which would mushroom into devastating propaganda campaigns.

If Enrique's Granadan actions were modestly successful, the subsidiary benefits he derived from them were signally important. He came to the throne in 1454, the year after the Ottoman Turks had taken Constantinople. Popes Nicholas V and Calixtus III tried to enlist Castilian aid in a proposed western crusade to re-establish the Byzantines in their former capital. Enrique and his envoy—the able intellectual Rodrigo Sánchez de Arévalo—persuaded the pope (Calixtus by then) to excuse Castile from participation and to recognize the campaigns against Granada as a parallel crusade against the same Islamic menace. The pope was won over by the Castilian arguments and granted the same privileges to those fighting in the Granadan war as those who were going to the east, while the crown was to receive income from the sale of indulgences. In this way Enrique avoided a costly foreign venture in the eastern Mediterranean and gained considerable income from the papal bulls of crusade granted to Castile. Enrique also used his selective reconquest to establish for himself a standing army, composed of 3,000 *lanzas* and 20,000 foot soldiers, to be paid for partly by subsidies from the Cortes and from the income of bulls of crusade. Such a permanent military force was a hallmark of the early modern monarchies and could be used for action against rebellious nobles as well as for service in Andalusia. The king did not derive maximum benefit from the standing army and its numbers never reached the authorized figures, but Fernando and Isabel made a firm reality of his beginnings.

24. Miguel Angel Ladero Quesada, *La hacienda real de Castilla en el siglo XV* (La Laguna, 1973), pp. 222–25, 244–45.

Enrique obtained for himself the masterships of the military orders of Santiago and Alcántara from Calixtus III, an achievement usually credited to Fernando and Isabel. The pope issued a bull granting him the position of master general of Santiago for fifteen years and that of Alcántara for ten. As head of the orders, Enrique enjoyed full temporal and limited spiritual powers over them and could appoint proxies to govern in his stead. His control of the military orders, with their large incomes and armed forces, enormously strengthened his power. Unfortunately, he delegated authority to men he believed to be trustworthy but who, he discovered, would not always accept his direction.[25]

Consideration of the monarch's disposition of the newly reconquered Gibraltar offers both indications of his ideas on royal control and the problems he faced with a recalcitrant aristocracy. It was also an anticipation of Castilian policies toward newly conquered areas overseas. In the fifteenth century two families of *grandes* struggled for supremacy in southern Andalusia: the Guzmanes, counts of Niebla and dukes of Medina Sidonia, and the Ponces de León, who possessed the county of Arcos. In 1462 Juan de Guzmán conquered Gibraltar and immediately found his possession contested by the count of Arcos. To settle the dispute, Enrique IV, before the end of the year, simply took over the territory for the crown and named Pedro de Porras temporary royal governor. In the next year Beltrán de la Cueva, in the midst of his rise in the king's favor, gained title to Gibraltar, to the intense annoyance of the Guzmán family. Accordingly, when a portion of the nobility began a revolt by raising Enrique's half brother Alfonso as rival king in Avila in 1465, Juan de Guzmán joined the rebels and secured Alfonso's permission to hold Gibraltar after his son Enrique recaptured it in 1467. Juan de Guzmán died the following year and control of Gibraltar passed to Enrique de Guzmán. Since Alfonso died about the same time, the new duke of Medina Sidonia petitioned Enrique IV to grant him title to the small but important territory. The king was concilia-

25. On the benefits derived from Enrique's Granadan policy, see Luis Suárez Fernández, "Los Trastámaras de Castilla y Aragón en el siglo XV (1407-74)," in vol. 15 of *Historia de España*, ed. Ramón Menéndez Pidal (Madrid, 1964), pp. 225–26; Richard H. Trame, *Rodrigo Sánchez de Arévalo, 1404-1470: Spanish Diplomat and Champion of the Papacy* (Washington, D.C., 1958), pp. 84–86; Eloy Benito Ruano, "Granada o Constantinopla," *Hispania* 20(1960):267–314. For a study of the bulls of crusade, see José Goñi Gaztambide, *Historia de la bula de cruzada en España* (Vitoria, 1958). The *lanzas* mentioned were mounted knights, with perhaps one attendant, unlike "lances" in France or Burgundy, which were composed of a knight, four other mounted soldiers, and various footmen: Ladero Quesada, *Castilla y la conquista*, pp. 13–14.

tory, and to bring the Guzmanes back to allegiance, he granted the duke's request, but the manner in which the grant was made indicated that Enrique IV wished to preserve sovereign rights for the crown. The duke of Medina Sidonia got control, but he and his heirs were forbidden to transfer title to any foreigner, cleric, or ecclesiastical order. The Castilian crown retained rights of taxation, coinage, and mineral rights (especially gold and silver), and, most important, military activity was a royal prerogative.[26]

In economic matters Enrique offered new approaches. Wool was the base of the Castilian export economy and was extremely lucrative for the producers, but its sale was too narrow a base to allow continuing economic stature in a Europe that was experiencing growth in manufactures. Textile production was creating prosperity in Flanders and Italy, and Castile would not be able to preserve prosperity on the basis of exports of raw materials alone. Accordingly, on the advice of the fledgling cloth manufacturers in Castile, and with the full support of the Cortes, in 1462 Enrique IV ordered that one-third of the annual production of raw wool should be retained in the kingdom for the use of the domestic cloth manufacturers. Enrique could well have had a double purpose in his action, since it would have sharply reduced the revenues of the nobility, and throughout his reign the greater nobility presented him with his gravest political difficulties. The policy did not work well, however, because the nobility and the Mesta they controlled used the turmoil of the later years of his reign to avoid compliance.[27] His successors did not maintain his wise policy. While they kept Enrique's legislation on the books, the *Reyes Católicos* capitulated to noble interests in this respect. They favored the Mesta over all other sectors of the economy—neglecting agriculture and industry—and laid the foundations for a precarious prosperity which would not last through the sixteenth century.

The king's interest in the Castilian economy included the great merchant fairs, which he rightly saw as the lifeline of the kingdom's commerce. He planned to establish a market fair in Segovia (which was the king's property) to rival those of Medina del Campo and other cities, thus divert-

26. J.L. Cano de Gardoqui and A. de Bethencourt, "Incorporación de Gibraltar a la Corona de Castilla (1438-1508)," *Hispania* 26 (1966):324–81.

27. Ramón Carande, *Siete estudios de historia de España* (Barcelona, 1969), pp. 14–17; Santiago Sobrequés, "La época del patriciado urbano," in vol. 2 of *Historia social y económica de España y América*, ed. Jaime Vicens Vives (Barcelona, 1957), p. 292; María del Carmen Carlé, "Mercaderes en Castilla (1252-1512)," *Cuadernos de Historia de España* 21–22 (1954):197. See the request of the Cortes at Toledo in 1462 and Enrique's response in *Cortes*, vol. 3, pp. 721–24.

ing some of their wealth to Segovia and bringing additional income to the royal treasury. Although Segovia's fair never became a major one, the king's plans for it were comprehensive. Enrique prepared a detailed plan of operation and even served as his own advertising agent by writing letters to the cities of the kingdom to ensure that the local officials would publicize the fairs to the utmost. He proposed that fairs be held twice a year in Segovia, each one lasting twenty days. Those who wished to attend were guaranteed safe conduct coming and going. All transactions were to be free of taxes and imposts, except for a specified list of items.[28]

In other economic matters Enrique clearly anticipated his successors; one of these was the problem of coinage. Throughout the fifteenth century, Castile had a steadily worsening monetary crisis, and inflation increased drastically. The coinage was steadily debased, both by royal initiative and by the huge number of private mints—quasi-legal as well as actual counterfeiting establishments. Enrique recognized the problem and in 1470 requested the cities to send advisers knowledgeable in coinage to meet with the Cortes and the royal council to draft a series of reforms. The outcome of their work was the pragmatic that the king signed in the Cortes of Segovia on 10 April 1471. These reforms demanded the closing of all the mints (perhaps 150) except the six traditional royal ones: Burgos, Cuenca, La Coruña, Segovia, Seville, and Toledo. Those remaining were to be organized under private management, but closely monitored by crown agents. The legislation provided carefully drafted schedules of wages for the mint workers and established the fees the operators could charge for coinage. Safeguards on the quality of the coins produced were to be the responsibility of all concerned. In this, as with so many of the king's quite commendable ideas, Enrique was unable to convert plans into practice, and the attempt at coinage reform had very little success.[29] The Catholic monarchs ultimately carried out a very similar reform of the coinage, no doubt inspired by the pragmatic of 1471.

In certain respects, Enrique IV can be counted among the founders of the Spanish system of taxation. An important source of royal income in

28. Enrique IV, letters to Murcia and Cartagena, 27 November 1459, printed in Juan Torres Fontes, *Estudio sobre la "Crónica de Enrique IV" del Dr. Galíndez de Carvajal* (Murcia, 1946), appended document 19, pp. 477–79.

29. AGS, *Diversos de Castilla, leg.* 4, fol. 27; Earl J. Hamilton, *American Treasure and the Price Revolution in Spain, 1501-1650* (Cambridge, Mass., 1934; repr. New York, 1965), pp. 47–50. Documents dealing with coinage reform appear in *Colección diplomática*, docs. 182–83, 185, 188. The coinage legislation of 1471 also appears in *Cortes*, vol. 3, article 26, pp. 812–34.

the fifteenth century was the *alcabala*, a sales tax of between five and ten percent levied on virtually all wholesale and retail exchanges of commodities, raw materials, manufactured goods, and livestock, and even on the transfer of real property. The tax originated in the thirteenth century, and throughout the Trastámara period of the late fourteenth and fifteenth centuries Castilian kings continually broadened its coverage and perfected the methods of its collection. In 1462 Enrique IV published his decrees on the administration of the tax in the *Cuaderno de alcabalas*, which reveals the fiscal sagacity of the monarch and his advisers and their desire to increase royal power and income. The *Cuaderno* is a well reasoned and detailed document which is closely followed in the taxation decrees of Isabel's reign. Enrique IV indicated the transactions which were subject to the *alcabala* and the means by which the tax was to be collected, taking care to ensure that the nobles and clergy paid the tax and that fraud and avoidance of payment were closely monitored. As examples, there were prohibitions on night sales and transactions outside the customary places of sale, while collectors were to maintain scales in public places and could have traffic watched to discover potential violators. The degree forbade fairs and markets in seigneurial areas, but the nobles probably could evade this stipulation. In the ordering of the tax structure of Castile, Enrique's legislation indicates that his government attempted to make the *alcabala* independent of control by the Cortes and to turn it into an ordinary source of revenue which did not have to be periodically renewed. But if he succeeded in one aspect, Enrique failed in another; many nobles secured the right to collect the *alcabala* in their jurisdictions.[30]

Enrique partially succeeded in another attempt at governmental regulation of the economy. In the face of appeals from the Cortes to regularize the widely varying systems of weights and measures in the towns and cities of Castile, in 1462 he delegated a group of royal inspectors to enforce a standardized plan of weights and measures. Again this was only a beginning, and the very restricted obedience to the monarch's dictates meant that full implementation was left to his successors.[31]

One of Enrique's clearest anticipations was the Santa Hermandad, the kingdom-wide organization of the previously local police brotherhoods

30. For a detailed discussion of this matter, see Salvador de Moxó, "Los Cuadernos de alcabalas: Orígenes de la legislación tributaria castellana," *Anuario de historia de derecho español* 39 (1969):317–67, especially pp. 325–27, 333, 341, 348–49, 352, 367; Ladero Quesada, *Hacienda real*, pp. 61–93.

31. Hamilton, *American Treasure*, pp. 156, 160.

(*Hermandades*). Although a truly national organization was only created in the last year of his reign, from at least 1456 Enrique worked for co-ordination of local units into larger entities. As in so many other aspects of Enrique's reign, we are forced to deduce royal actions from incomplete records. In this case, our earliest evidence comes from a 1456 document from the town archive of Espinar in Segovia province.[32] In this letter from the city council of Segovia to the town council of Espinar, we can see Enrique's orders at work. First he decreed that Segovia join a combined *Hermandad* together with Burgos, Avila, Palencia, Valladolid, Arévalo, Roa, and Aranda, thus covering a large portion of Old Castile. The directors of this organization—all royal appointees—were Pedro de Luxán, *asistente* (an office similar to that of *corregidor*) in Burgos, Diego de Aguila, Gonzalo Mexía, and Juan de Porras, *corregidores* in Segovia, Valladolid, and Avila respectively. They in turn decided that each town in the region should send troopers (*cuadrilleros*) to serve in the forces of the main city. Towns of forty inhabitants and above were to send two troopers, others, one, in order that "evildoers and delinquents will be more closely pursued and captured."[33]

Fragmentary references show that Enrique was concerned with more than just this area. In 1459 he insisted that San Sebastián should send citizens to aid the *Hermandades*.[34] In 1464 he ordered that Madrid join with Segovia in the co-ordination of their *Hermandades*. The same year he commanded Cuenca to form a *Hermandad* with Huete, Ucles, Requena, Moya, and Huélamo; this unit was to be directed by the king's former tutor Lope Barrientos.[35] When the civil war broke out in 1465 he got immediate aid from these militias, and in 1466 a "junta general de la Hermandad" met in the village of Santa Olalla.[36] Although our evidence is slight, we must conclude from the chronicle of Palencia—a rebel partisan—

32. RAH, *Colección general de Cortes, leyes, fueros, privilegios, y otros documentos* (known as *Colección Salvá*, call number 9/4278), vol. 15, pp. 42r–43r. Palencia, *Crónica*, 1:191–92, reports that the co-ordination of the local *Hermandades* began in 1465 or 1466. He was hostile to Enrique, and this fact may have contributed to his assertions. A recent study of the background of the Santa Hermandad is María del Carmen Pescador del Hoyo, "Los orígenes de la Santa Hermandad," *Cuadernos de historia de España* 55–56 (1972):400–443. On pp. 442–43 she shows that one of the local groups, the "Vieja y Santa Hermanded de Toledo, Talavera, y Ciudad Real," gave its allegiance to the rebels in 1465.
33. RAH, *Salvá*, vol. 15, p. 43r.
34. Torres Fontes, *Itinerario*, p. 98. The date is 15 April 1459.
35. Ibid., pp. 160–61.
36. Ibid., p. 197.

that the forces in revolt against the king felt a real threat from the *Hermandades.*[37]

The full national organization emerged in the last year of Enrique's reign when "constitutions" were made for the government of the general *Hermandad.*[38] Fernando and Isabel made great use of this restructured organization, creating a central council for it and using its troops in defense against the Portuguese invasion and the subsequent Granadan war,[39] but the basis was set by their predecessor.

For an assessment of the early phase of Enrique's reign, we have a revealing passage from his court chronicler:

> Great praises for a magnificient prince had the king in those days when his affairs went prosperously. For while fortune was favorable to him and not contrary; very famous acts and signal works of greatness were his, from which he merited clear renown among the kings of his time. And not without reason, for he had in his personal guard 3,600 *lanzas*, men of arms, and geneters, with many outstanding captains. In his court were many noble sons of *grandes*, and other notable and honorable persons. . . . He was very much loved by the good and feared by the bad, and served by his followers, but in secret poorly loved by the *grandes*. . . . He went around his kingdom very powerfully; all his followers rich, content, and desirous of his service; justice was well administered in his council, where the cases of his court were heard. And the chancellery, where pleas were carried, had presiding prelates [and] famous, conscientious *letrados*, where the truth was discovered, and for no reason was justice twisted.[40]

But fortune did become unfavorable and contrary. The foregoing pages clearly indicate the successes of Enrique IV, yet his reign experienced increasing political unrest. We must turn now to an examination of the discontent that would develop into open civil war.

37. Palencia, *Crónica*, 1:210.

38. Torres Fontes, *Itinerario*, p. 260.

39. Marvin Lunenfeld, *The Council of the Santa Hermandad: A Study of the Pacification Forces of Ferdinand and Isabella* (Coral Gables, Florida, 1970).

40. Enríquez, *Crónica*, pp. 110–11. He was not exaggerating. Tarsicio de Azcona, *Isabel la Católica: Estudio crítico de su vida y su reinado* (Madrid, 1964), pp. 53–57, reports the sworn testimony of many notables in a legal case during 1480–83. All regarded the first decade of Enrique's rule as peaceful and just.

V

THE DRIFT TOWARD CIVIL WAR

Even as Enrique IV was making a promising beginning in his reign, a nucleus of opposition began to form. As they watched the policies of the new king unfold, certain nobles became increasingly restive. Since they considered themselves the traditional advisers and arbiters of the crown, their cardinal fear was that an aggressive royal government would encroach on their prerogatives and reduce the scope of their action. Recalling their difficulties with Alvaro de Luna, some were apprehensive about Juan Pacheco's apparent power. Many nobles did not understand the king's strategy of limited warfare on the Granadan front and clamored for an unrestrained attack on the Muslim kingdom, believing that this would allow them greater possibilities to secure wealth and booty for themselves and lands for their younger sons. They were not comforted by the king's assumption of the masterships of the military orders and his intended creation of a standing army. In addition, they resented the rise of new men in the royal entourage.

At a distance of five centuries and from the vantage point of a society whose distinctions are based on wealth and influence, it is almost impossible for us to imagine the noble mentality, particularly noble resentment over the rise of new men. Two possible motives for the nobles' dislike could have been at play: scorn for upstarts because of their birth, or hostility because such men were coming to exclude others from their accustomed advisory roles.[1]

For whatever reason, the most distrusted of the new men was Juan Pacheco, the marquis of Villena. During most of the reign the most important person next to the king, Pacheco's continual aim was to establish himself as the dominant figure in the realm and to advance his family's fortunes. Through his brother Pedro Girón's control of the military order of Calatrava, and because Enrique in 1456 had given Girón control over the frontier of

1. Chroniclers characterize many of Enrique's followers as "de poco estado" or "de bajo linaje." Whether such tags suggest scorn or are merely descriptive is impossible to tell.

Granada, Pacheco had a ready source of income and troops to supplement his own. He was a persuasive speaker and a convincing debater, although he had a slightly tremulous voice.[2] His was the hand behind most of Enrique's political manuevers during the principate, and although the mature king could more easily resist Pacheco's attempts at dictating policy, Enrique could not succeed in ridding himself completely of the influence of the marquis. As always, Pacheco can be seen constantly in action, stirring up trouble, working to aid the king against noble leagues, or lending the leagues his support. His whole policy seemed to be directed toward keeping the kingdom in a state of unrest and using the unrest he helped create to advance his own power and wealth. To Enrique's credit he resisted Pacheco, but not forcefully enough or often enough.

Pacheco received sporadic aid from his irascible uncle Alfonso Carrillo, the archbishop of Toledo since 1445, who was to be a pivotal, though inconstant, figure throughout Enrique's reign. Born in Cuenca in 1412, Carrillo had relatives in high ecclesiastical positions, most notably his uncle, also named Alfonso Carrillo, who became a cardinal under Pope Benedict XIII. The young Carrillo accompanied his uncle to various clerical deliberations in Rome, Bologna, Basle, and Avignon. But despite the time he spent in high church circles, the future Toledan archbishop was completely untouched by the intellectual currents of either the Middle Ages or the Renaissance–except for alchemy–and remained to the end a warrior-bishop more suited to battle and political intrigue than to intellectual speculation.[3]

By 1457 Pacheco had established himself in a very powerful position in the royal government. He had joined an aristocratic plot directed by Alfonso Carrillo together with the admiral Fadrique Enríquez, the marquis of Santillana, and the counts of Alba, Haro, and Benavente. Using this league as a pretext, Pacheco convinced Enrique of the necessity for a countervailing force, composed of his brother Girón, Lope Barrientos, Archbishop Fonseca of Seville, Alfonso Pimentel, Alvaro de Stúñiga, and Diego Arias de Avila, with Pacheco of course at its head. The king undertook an agreement with this group in March 1457, a very significant act

2. Fernando del Pulgar, *Claros varones de Castilla*, ed. R.B. Tate (Oxford, 1971), p. 30, stated that the speech defect was accidental. Alonso de Palencia, *Crónica de Enrique IV*, trans. Antonio Paz y Meliá, 2 vols., in *Biblioteca de autores españoles* 207–208 (Madrid, 1973-75), 1:76, said that it was natural and that Pacheco's wife affected to imitate him.

3. Francisco Esteve Barba, *Alfonso Carrillo de Acuña: Autor de la unidad de España* (Madrid, 1943), pp. 2–6.

as it turned out. Pacheco got control of the Consejo and for some six years occupied such an exalted position that the period from 1457 to 1463 has been called the government of Pacheco. Even more significant was the fact that Enrique was reduced to openly playing partisan politics.[4] From 1458, Pacheco's maneuvers for increasing his personal estate, coupled with Enrique's limited prosecution of the Granadan war, inspired even greater disaffection on the part of the nobles opposed to the king and started the chain of events which plunged Castile into civil war in the second half of Enrique's reign.

In 1458 and 1459 Pacheco provoked two major changes in the circle of Enrique's close associates. Although even the canny Pacheco could not foresee it, the changes would lead to his being pushed from the circle himself. His first move was to oust Miguel Lucas de Iranzo. Very soon after the brilliant celebrations in Madrid when Lucas was created a noble and given many offices, including that of constable,[5] Pacheco, Lucas's chronicler tells us, felt the grip of jealousy and fear and persuaded Enrique to withhold some promised grants from Lucas. The constable then fled the court and ended up in self-imposed exile in Jaén, where he remained until the end of his life.[6] In the course of these machinations, Pacheco engineered the rise of Beltrán de la Cueva in royal favor.[7] At about the same time, estrangement between the crown and the powerful Mendoza family almost reached open war. The Mendozas were already angry since Pacheco had taken over lands abutting their holdings around Guadalajara, and the king was abetting anti-Mendoza elements in the city of Guadalajara.[8] As a result, there were strained relations for several years.

Alfonso V of Aragon died in 1458 and was succeeded by Juan II, *de facto* king of Navarre. At the beginning there was a superficial friendship between Enrique and Juan, although harmony would soon dissipate as

4. The agreement with the Pacheco cabal is in AGS, *Diversos de Castilla, leg.* 9, fol. 32. The phrase "the government of Pacheco" is adapted from Luis Suárez Fernández, *Nobleza y monarquía: Puntos de vista sobre la historia castellana del siglo XV*, 2nd ed. (Valladolid, 1975), p. 190.

5. *Hechos del Condestable Don Miguel Lucas de Iranzo*, ed. Juan de Mata Carriazo, Colección de crónicas españoles, no. 3 (Madrid, 1941), pp. 3-13.

6. Ibid., pp. 13-27. Palencia, always trying to put the worst possible face on Enrique's actions, suggested that Lucas left the court as the result of a homosexual tiff: *Crónica*, 1:106.

7. J.F. O'Callaghan, "Don Pedro Girón: Master of the Order of Calatrava," *Hispania* 21 (1961):373.

8. Francisco Layna Serrano, *Historia de Guadalajara y sus Mendozas en los siglos XV y XVI*, 4 vols. (Madrid, 1942), 2:104-105.

Juan II of Aragon revealed himself as Enrique's greatest antagonist. Early in the reign they negotiated a double marriage to join Enrique's half-siblings Alfonso and Isabel with Juan's children Leonor and Fernando. Certain nobles were upset by the implied cordiality of the two kings, fearing the Aragonese. They were even more annoyed in 1460 when Pacheco obtained Enrique's permission to attack the marquis of Santillana and Pedro González de Mendoza because of their entry into a plot with the count of Alba to overthrow Pacheco's hold on the royal government.[9]

Faced with these actions, Carrillo obtained the adherence of a good part of the ranking nobility to a league ostensibly directed to the good of the kingdom, at Alcalá de Henares in March 1460. In addition to Carrillo, the league was composed of Santillana, Fadrique, and the counts of Alba, Haro, Benavente, Plasencia, and Alba de Liste. The aims of the league were to have Alfonso named heir to the throne and to secure for themselves control of the Consejo. By the beginning of April they got Juan II of Aragon to lend his support in an agreement reached at Tudela. Pacheco watched the developments with interest and delegated Pedro Girón to keep his personal communications open with the league. Juan's action infuriated Enrique, and the Castilian king decided to attack the Aragonese monarch by throwing his support to Carlos de Viana.[10]

Prince Carlos was the son of Juan by his first marriage with Queen Blanca of Navarre and was legally the king of Navarre. His sister was Blanca, first wife of Enrique IV. He enjoyed almost boundless personal popularity in the kingdoms of the Crown of Aragon. His greatest enemy was his stepmother Juana, daughter of the Castilian admiral Fadrique Enríquez. Juana was anxious to exclude Carlos from the line of succession in order to provide for her son Fernando. Through complicated and lengthy diplomatic persuasion, by December 1460 Enrique of Castile was able to thwart her plans and achieve his own. He got from Carlos de Viana a preliminary agreement of marriage with Isabel and acceptance of Castilian aid in asserting his position against his father and stepmother. Pacheco, following his own ends, got word of the secret agreement to the noble league, and Fadrique informed his daughter, who persuaded her husband Juan II to imprison Carlos.[11]

9. Suárez, *Nobleza y monarquía*, p. 194.

10. Ibid.; Jaime Vicens Vives, *Historia crítica de la vida y reinado de Fernando II de Aragón* (Zaragoza, 1962), p. 213.

11. Diego Enríquez del Castillo, *Crónica del rey Don Enrique el cuarto de este nombre*, ed. Cayetano Rosell, in vol. 70 of *Biblioteca de autores españoles* (Madrid, 1953), pp. 114–15.

The problems of Carlos de Viana transcended a mere family dispute involving a wicked stepmother and a cruel father; they intermingled with very basic concerns of both Navarre and Catalonia and their relations with Juan II of Aragon. For many of the Navarrese, Viana represented a hope of independence from the centripetal atttraction of the increasingly centralized Crown of Aragon and its ambitious king. Navarre was divided into upper and lower regions. *Alta* Navarre was a Basque-speaking, pastoral area, linked economically with the Castilian wool trade; dominant politically was the Beaumont family. *Baja* Navarre, led by the Agramont family, was Castilian-speaking; its more highly developed agriculture and commerce impelled it toward the Mediterranean ambit of the Crown of Aragon. Carlos fell under the sway of the Beaumont faction, particularly because of his tutor and later counsellor Juan de Beaumont, prior of the Navarrese section of the order of St. John of Jerusalem. Because of the economic orientation of upper Navarre, and since he wished to prevent his father from using Navarre as a pawn in his wider schemes, Viana found himself driven toward diplomatic agreement with Enrique IV.[12]

Enrique then began preparations for a war against Aragon, and Pacheco persuaded him to settle differences with his own nobles before he attempted such a formidable task. Pacheco and Girón were charged with working out an agreement with the nobles of the league to obtain troops to be used in the war in Navarre. In return the crown promised to meet later with the nobles to work out a reshuffle of the Consejo, guarantees of noble prerogatives, and the naming of Alfonso as heir.[13]

When Enrique got word of the imprisonment of Carlos de Viana in January 1461, he sent Pedro Girón and Gonzalo de Saavedra with a mounted force of 1,500 into Navarre to aid the prince. The Castilian troops were immediately successful both in Navarre and along the Aragonese-Castilian border. Early in March the news reached Castile that Carlos had been freed and Enrique moved close to the border to direct operations personally. By this time his differences with the league of nobles had disappeared for the moment. Carlos then undertook a diplomatic move which annoyed the Castilian king: he opened negotiations with the French dauphin Louis. To Enrique, this seemed to prejudice the Castilian-French alliance, since it was in part contrary to the diplomacy of Charles VII, Louis's father, although Carlos de Viana was more concerned with protecting his

12. Jaime Vicens Vives, *Juan II de Aragón (1398-1479): Monarquía y revolución en la España del siglo XV* (Barcelona, 1953), pp. 141-51, 157-59.

13. *Colección diplomática*, doc. 67.

position than with adapting himself to Enrique's foreign policy. On the military front the Castilians continued their successes. By early summer they had captured a number of towns and placed Carlos in a strong enough position to work out an agreement with his father at Villafranca. The Catalans had also risen in favor of Carlos, and in June at Villafranca Juan II named Carlos *lugarteniente* in Catalonia with wide powers. A commission was appointed to work out peace terms between Castile and Aragon, and Juan and Enrique signed the agreement on 26 August 1461.[14]

On that same day Enrique gave in to the demands of the rebel junta as he had promised in principle to do earlier in the year. At this point the king sought an end to the problems he had been forced to cope with, but it is almost impossible to see why he had to capitulate completely. It was certainly a mistake. He may have believed that he could solve his difficulties simply by giving in to the demands, yet the domestic peace he secured was both costly and illusory. In its widest connotations, Enrique's capitulation was a victory for the dissidents; thereafter they were able to influence the appointment of royal councillors. If they had continued to work together, Enrique's monarchy would have been a sham. The king's only remaining hope was to play off one group of nobles against the other. Many saw Enrique's dilemma as a chance to establish and enlarge their private domains. Pedro Girón, for example, used the confusion to found the house of Osuna for his three illegitimate sons. Thereafter, his family was to control a large area in Andalusia.[15]

The designation of Alfonso as royal heir was put in abeyance by the queen's giving birth to a daughter—Juana—on 28 February 1462, a momentous event for Castile. The chroniclers mention rejoicing on the part of the king and his subjects. Although much was to be made later of the supposed illegitimacy of Juana, at the time of her birth it is vitually certain that no rumors existed. Alfonso Carrillo, the archbishop of Toledo and primate of Castile, bapitized the princess, the same Carrillo who the year previously had been leading the league against Enrique. Soon afterwards the Cortes recognized Juana as the heir to the crown of Castile. French

14. Angel Canellas López, "El reino de Aragón en el siglo XV (1410-79)," in vol. 15 of *Historia de España*, ed. Ramón Menéndez Pidal (Madrid, 1964), p. 438; Jaime Vicens Vives, "Los Trastámaras y Cataluña," in ibid., pp. 765–68; Luis Suárez Fernández, "Los Trastámaras de Castilla y Aragón en el siglo XV (1407-74)," in ibid., pp. 237–39; O'Callaghan, "Don Pedro Girón," pp. 371–72. The agreement between Enrique and Carrillo's faction of 5 May 1461 is printed in *Colección diplomática*, doc. 67.

15. Suárez, "Los Trastámaras," pp. 230–40; O'Callaghan, "Don Pedro Girón," p. 373.

and Portuguese envoys present at the Castilian court found no cause to doubt Juana's legitimacy. At the beginning there were no questions as to the legality of her position; those were to arise later in the political machinations of the civil war.[16]

Much has been written by hostile chroniclers and historians of the shabby treatment that the king was supposed to have accorded his half sister and brother Isabel and Alfonso. He was accused of keeping them prisoners in near poverty and housed in isolated castles until the birth of Juana, and thereafter maintaining them under close supervision in the royal household to keep the nobles from giving them aid. In fact, according to the chronicler Enríquez del Castillo, the king provided for the young *infantes* in a manner suitable to their rank, allowing them a permanent residence to spare them the hardship of life in an ambulatory court. After Juana's birth, as Enríquez stated, the nobles themselves petitioned the king to allow the *infantes* to live in the king's household, citing as reasons the benefits they could derive from associations with those in high places.[17] Obviously the nobles at this time did not consider the royal household a den of vice and loose living, as they were later to claim.

In a move which could account for the later belief that Enrique thought Beltrán de la Cueva to be the actual father of Juana, shortly after the birth the king awarded the countship of Ledesma to his favorite and staunchest supporter. At the same time, Enrique used the advancement of Beltrán to give his former position of *mayordomo mayor* to another new man of middling background but great loyalty—Andrés Cabrera.[18]

Somewhat overshadowed by the birth of the royal daughter, the questions of involvement in Aragon kept the diplomatic waters stirred during late 1461 and early 1462. Shortly after Carlos de Viana had accepted the agreement of Villafranca with his father, he died in Barcelona (23 September 1461). Under the terms of the Villafranca pact, Juan installed his son Fernando as *lugarteniente* of Catalonia, with his mother Juana serving as his "tutor" (*tudriu*). Fernando, then nine years old, took up residence in

16. Enríquez, *Crónica*, pp. 120–21; Palencia, *Crónica*, 1:132–33. The exact date of Juana's recognition as heir is unclear, but by mid-May 1462 the king had written to Rodrigo Pimentel stating that the act had been done, AHN, *Osuna*, *leg*. 419, fol. 361. Queen Juana wrote to Seville on 7 March 1462 announcing the birth. BN, Ms. 2993, no. 6, fol. 13v.

17. Enríquez, *Crónica*, pp. 119–20.

18. Ibid., p. 120. In addition to the title, Beltrán got the town of Ledesma: Juan Torres Fontes, *Itinerario de Enrique IV de Castilla* (Murcia, 1955), p. 126. Cabrera's grant is in AGS, *Quitaciones de Corte*, *leg*. 2.

Barcelona in November 1461, but nothing the royal family could do was able to stem the growing surge of rebellion. For over half a year the Catalans prepared to assert themselves, and in August 1462 they offered Enrique the Crown of Aragon, even though they could really speak only for Catalonia. Enrique moved quickly and sent troops in to assist the Catalans in resistance to the siege of Barcelona which Juan had begun. By late in the year Enrique had gathered a large army for a full-scale invasion and through his agents he had been arousing anti-royal elements throughout Aragon.[19] Enrique, taking the Catalan titles "comte de Barcelona i senyor del Principat de Catalunya," appointed Juan de Beaumont, the former counsellor of Carlos de Viana and leader of the Beaumont faction in Navarre, as his *lugarteniente general* (chief lieutenant) in Catalonia.[20]

Enrique's Catalan intervention was ill fated from the start. First of all, Louis XI of France was playing a double diplomatic game. He was in negotiation with Juan II, agreeing to provide French forces to aid Juan against the Catalans in return for cession of Roussillon and Cerdagne and part of Navarre.[21] Meanwhile, he was in contact with Castile about a project for the marriage of Charles, the duke of Berry and brother of Louis, and Isabel—the perennial diplomatic pawn. The couple were supposedly to be given dominion over Catalonia. At home in Castile, Carrillo and Pacheco were working together for the moment. They seemed to fear the prestige Enrique would enjoy if his Aragonese adventure were to turn out as successfully as it seemed it would. Therefore they sought ways of averting a royal victory, recognizing the threat a victorious king would pose to themselves and their followers.

In Navarre Juan II's machinations brought about a curious episode. By his first marriage to Queen Blanca de Navarra, Juan had assumed title to the Navarrese throne, but constitutionally it was not his. Legally the crown passed to the heirs of his marriage—his son Carlos de Viana and his daughters Blanca and Leonor. Carlos was now dead, Blanca was divorced from Enrique IV, and Leonor was married to the French nobleman Gaston

19. Enríquez, *Crónica*, pp. 122–25; Vicens, "Los Trastámaras y Cataluña," pp. 768–70; Canellas, "Reino de Aragón," p. 443; *Colección diplomática*, docs. 77–78.
20. ACA, *Cancilleria, Intrusos, libro* 1, fol. 1; Vicens, *Juan II de Aragón*, p. 273. Jaime Sobrequés Callicó, "Enric IV de Castella, senyor del principat de Catalunya," in vol. 1 of *La guerra civil catalana del segle XV*, ed. S. Sobrequés (Barcelona, 1973), pp. 357–58. The registry of Beaumont's chancellery documents is provided by Jaime Sobrequés Callicó, *Catálogo de la cancillería de Enrique IV de Castilla, señor del principado de Cataluña (Lugartenencia de Juan de Beaumont, 1462-1464)* (Barcelona, 1975).
21. Vicens, "Los Trastámaras y Cataluña," pp. 770–72; Vicens, Fernando II, p. 216.

de Foix. To placate Louis XI, Juan conceived a plot to give Gaston control of Navarre by passing over Blanca. She was virtually held a prisoner while Gaston asserted his control over the kingdom. But Blanca, who was to die very shortly, on 30 April 1462 renounced all her rights in Navarre, including her right to the throne, to Enrique of Castile, her former husband. This gave Enrique an interesting claim and a pretext for expansion into Navarre, if he had been willing and able to assert it.[22]

Late in 1462 the Catalans reiterated their offer of the Crown of Aragon to Enrique and urged him to come in person to accept it. Carrillo and Pacheco, almost surely under the influence of Louis XI and definitely in contact with the Aragonese queen, persuaded Enrique to meet with the French king and allow him to arbitrate the differences between Castile and Aragon. They used an economic argument: intervention in Aragon would be expensive and Castile was in no way able to afford it with the treasury weak and inflation rampant. Events beyond Enrique's control also compelled him to seek a negotiated settlement in Catalonia. In January of 1463 Perpignan on the Franco-Catalan frontier fell with heavy losses of artillery and powder. Its loss increased the French threat to other border provinces and indeed all Catalonia. Pacheco and Carrillo kept up their pressure, and by April of that year Enrique was willing to meet with Louis XI.[23]

Accordingly the kings of France and Castile held an interview on the Bidassoa River, the division between their two kingdoms. In the course of a long conversation, Enrique agreed to withdraw his support of the rebellious Catalans, remove his forces from Aragonese territory, and drop his claim to the crown. Louis awarded Enrique the Navarrese town of Estella and its surrounding hinterland (*y su merindad*) in compensation and asserted that Juan II would undertake to respect the constitutional claims of the Catalans. Commentators have generally considered that Enrique lost a great deal in his negotiations with Louis XI, but that interpretation needs reconsideration. In return for renouncing a tenuous claim to the Aragonese throne and a precarious sovereignty in Catalonia, which was divided from Castile by hostile territory, Enrique gained a firm claim on Estella, one of the six

22. Suárez, "Los Trastámaras," pp. 241–42; Orestes Ferrara, *Un pleito sucesorio: Enrique IV, Isabel de Castilla y La Beltraneja* (Madrid, 1945), pp. 72–81. The original document is in AGS, *Patronato Real, leg.* 12, fols. 11–12; printed in *Codoin*, 41:27, and *Colección diplomática*, doc. 73. Blanca's protests about her father's treatment can be seen in *Colección diplomática*, docs. 70–72.

23. Vicens, 'Los Trastámaras y Cataluña," p. 772; Enríquez, *Crónica*, pp. 125–28; *Colección diplomática*, docs. 75–82; Sobrequés Callicó, ed., *Catálogo de la cancillería*, doc. 331, p. 71.

merindades of Navarre, which was contiguous with Castile. Tired of politics and greatly angered by the discovery of Pacheco's treachery, Enrique retired to Segovia after the meeting with the French king.[24] As he relaxed in his favorite city and its nearby forests, he could take pleasure in the news that while he had been occupied with the Aragonese crisis Castilian forces in the south had taken Gibraltar and Archidona from the Muslims.[25]

With Pacheco and Carrillo in disgrace, the Mendozas consolidated their influence, became Enrique's strongest supporters, and worked closely with the king to give new life to the monarchy. The reconcilation between the Mendoza clan and the crown was accomplished by Pedro González de Mendoza, and his tool was Beltrán de la Cueva. The first provisional truce between the two groups had taken place in 1461, while Pacheco was still in the court and jealous of the rise of Beltrán's star. Pedro thereafter lived in the court and worked against Pacheco. The most important result of his stealthy, steady maneuvering was the marriage of Mencía de Mendoza, a younger daughter of Diego Hurtado de Mendoza (second marquis of Santillana after the death of his father in 1458), to Beltrán. After this alliance, the influence of the Mendozas and Beltrán waxed as Pacheco and his crew steadily withdrew into open antagonism.[26]

During the five years, 1460 to 1465, before the civil war broke out, Enrique made a number of concesssions designed to secure the allegiances

24. Enríquez, *Crónica*, pp. 128–29; Palencia, *Crónica*, 1:138–40; Vicens, *Juan II de Aragón*, p. 227; *Colección diplomática*, doc. 84. Document 87 of *Colección diplomática* is the secret agreement between Louis XI and Pacheco. Pacheco's second son was to wed a bastard daughter of the French king. For the French side see Thomas Basin, *Histoire de Louis XI*, 3 vols., ed. and trans. Charles Samaran and Monique-Cécile Garaud (Paris, 1963-72), 1:111; Philippe Commynes, *Memoirs: The Reign of Louis XI, 1461-83*, trans. Michael Jones (Harmondsworth, 1972), pp. 142–43. On the question of Estella, *Colección diplomática*, doc. 90. On the *merindades* of Navarre, see Luis G. de Valdeavellano, *Curso de historia de las instituciones españoles de los orígenes al final de la Edad Media*, 4th. ed. (Madrid, 1975), p. 511.

    Before the interview Beaumont, Enrique's lieutenant in Catalonia, wrote to the king requesting that he (Beaumont) be present during the talks and that Enrique make sure that the case of Blanca de Navarra be discussed. Beaumont also wrote to Pacheco, Carrillo, Alvaro Gómez, and Queen Juana to watch Enrique carefully and not to allow him to eat with the French king because of the danger of poisoning. Sobrequés Callicó, ed., *Catálogo de la cancillería*, docs. 467–70, p. 96.

25. Enríquez, *Crónica*, pp. 124–25.

26. Layna Serrano, *Guadalajara y sus Mendozas*, 2:114–16. AHN, *Osuna*, *leg.* 1860, fol. 10, contains Enrique's promise "to guard and honor Diego Hurtado de Mendoza in the same manner as the other *grandes*. . . ."

of influential *grandes*. The Portocarreros received grants: Rodrigo de Portocarrero (first count of Medellín) received the right to found a *mayorazgo* in 1460,[27] his successor Juan was named *repostero mayor* in 1463,[28] and Luis received the town of Hornachuelos.[29] Juan Ponce de León was licensed to create a *mayorazgo* in 1461[30] and made *alcalde mayor* of Seville in March 1465.[31] In January 1465 Enrique gave the castle of El Carpio to the count of Alba de Tormes, Garcí Alvarez de Toledo.[32] Diego Pérez Sarmiento (count of Salinas) received the income of the salt pans of Añana.[33] Two other counts received towns: Fernando de Rojas (count of Castro) received Herma, and Juan Pimentel (count of Benavente) received Barrios de Salas.[34] Not all those honored would remain loyal, but Enrique was doing what he could to secure support.

As the war approached, Enrique worked to consolidate his foregin relations on the south and west. In Jaén he signed a treaty with Granada. In Gibraltar he had a meeting with Afonso V of Portugal, and the two kings agreed to sign a treaty of friendship. They met again in April 1464 in the town of Puente del Arzobispo and agreed to a formal alliance. One topic of conversation was a possible marriage between Afonso of Portugal and Isabel. Enrique now had a firm foreign agreement to support him against the dissidents of his own kingdom and the king of Aragon.[35]

Carrillo and Pacheco were thoroughly convinced of the danger of Enrique's actions and felt it could not be long before he moved against them. Pacheco was extremely jealous of the regard Enrique had for Beltrán and the influence the Mendozas had gained, and he was angered at his own exclusion from the inner circle and at Enrique's coolness to Girón. Carrillo was much aroused over rumors of the Portuguese marriage and hoped to secure control of Alfonso, the young *infante*. With these fears in mind, the two convoked a meeting at Alcalá de Henares to communicate their concerns to others. Quickly, they got important adherents to the new league opposed to the king: Fadrique Enríquez, Rodrigo Pimentel, Iñigo Manrique, Alvaro de Stúñiga, and Garcí Alvarez de Toledo. The league's aim was to

27. RAH, *Salazar*, *leg.* M-90, *hojas* 320v–32v.
28. Ibid., *leg.* M-90, *hoja* 323v.
29. Ibid., *leg.* M-117, *hojas* 225–27.
30. Ibid., *leg.* M-43, fols. 187–88v.
31. Ibid., *leg.* B-3, fol. 362.
32. Torres Fontes, *Itinerario*, p. 169.
33. RAH, *Salazar*, *leg.* M-37, fols. 112–14v.
34. Benavente's grant: AHN, *Osuna*, *carpeta* 61, no. 16; Castro's grant: ibid., *leg.* 1965, fol. 1.
35. Enríquez, *Crónica*, pp. 131–32; Palencia, *Crónica*, 1:142–43, 146.

get control of the *infantes* Alfonso and Isabel and to use them as tools in the struggle.[36] The king of Aragon made a pact with them, but he was content to watch from the wings as the Castilian drama began.[37] Soon after the meeting, civil war broke out in earnest. Suárez Fernández has pointed out the interesting fact that at the beginning of the civil war Enrique's followers—the Mendozas and the Velascos—were also the staunchest supporters of the *Reyes Católicos* when they entered the arena, and that the same enemies were shared by Enrique and his successors: the Pachecos, Carrillo, and the Stúñigas.[38] Suárez believed that this indicated that the battle was between rival ideologies, not personalities. The Mendozas and the Velascos wanted a strong monarchy, it is true, partly to ensure that they maintained their position, but far more important was their distrust of their opponents. The Pachecos and the Stúñiga sought only a king they could control and who would allow them freedom of action to expand their authority; if not Enrique, then Alfonso. When Alfonso died, they first sounded out Isabel and then returned to Enrique and Juana.

In a carefully conceived act designed to strengthen his position, Enrique conferred the mastership of the order of Santiago on Beltrán de la Cueva, sending Suero de Solís to Rome to seek papal confirmation. Pacheco attempted to forestall the king and sent the chronicler Palencia to argue against Beltrán before the pope. Pacheco had consistently tried to get possession of the mastership for himself, or at least to prevent its passing to Beltrán. Therefore, to further counter Beltrán's appointment, he got the counts of Plasencia and Alba to propose a meeting between Enrique and the leaders of the league, to be held on 16 September 1464 in the country between San Pedro de las Dueñas and Villacastín. Enrique agreed to meet with the league, but as the appointed time drew near, ominous rumors reached the royal camp. On the fifteenth, Fadrique Enríquez attempted a premature uprising in Valladolid in favor of the *infante* Alfonso. As Enrique cautiously approached the appointed meeting place, a defector from the noble faction gave the king a last-minute warning that the nobles were mobilized and prepared to capture him. Ill-prepared, Enrique was saved from his difficult position only by the spontaneous outpouring of peasants and townsmen of the region, organized in their local *Hermandad*, who responded to the call of alarm and placed some 5,000 troops (if the figures of the chronicler can be credited) at the king's disposal. At the

36. Palencia, *Crónica*, 1:151–52; *Colección diplomática*, doc. 92.
37. Vicens, *Juan II de Aragón*, pp. 289–90.
38. Suárez, *Nobleza y monarquía*, p. 213.

beginning of armed hostilities Enrique could count on considerable popular support.[39]

Pacheco and Girón assembled their adherents in Burgos in late September 1464 and proclaimed that they were acting as the representatives of the three estates of the kingdom. Recognizing the necessity of winning popular support, they addressed a statement to all the cities of Castile in which they outlined their opposition in terms designed to appeal to the populace. The letter stated that the king showed favoritism to non-Christians (Jews and Muslims); he had relinquished royal power to Beltrán de la Cueva; his intervention in Catalonia had been illegal; his *corregidores* and other officials were acting illegally. Thus the noble manifesto carefully mixed real grievances with propaganda directed at the townspeople. The letter ended with a demand that Enrique proclaim Alfonso as his heir and that Beltrán should renounce the mastership of Santiago in favor of Alfonso.[40] It should be stressed that while Pacheco had always wanted the mastership for himself, he now realized that a demand for Alfonso to have it would have a greater propagandistic impact, and he could hope to gain control of the boy.

After his narrow escape from the noble ambush, Enrique retired to Valladolid, where he was when a copy of the aristocratic manifesto reached him. The advisers he assembled to discuss the royal response, especially Beltrán, Pedro González de Mendoza, and Lope Barrientos (bishop of Cuenca), were all for war. Barrientos put forth a strong argument in favor of it and assured the king of victory. His reasoning was a mixture of piety and economic determinism. Enrique would win because the rebels were traitors; therefore, God would favor the anointed king. In addition, the king was richer than the nobles, and victory would naturally go to the side with the larger purse. Enrique gave an equally interesting reply, one which showed his concern with the lives of his men—the same concern which had helped form his policy in the Granadan war. To Barrientos Enrique said:

> Do you wish, Father Bishop, that at all costs the battle should be fought, so that the people of both sides should perish? It seems clear that they are not your sons who will enter the fight, nor

39. *Crónica incompleta de los Reyes Católicos (1469-76)*, ed. Julio Puyol (Madrid, 1934), p. 58. Suárez, "Los Trastámaras," p. 258; Vicens, *Fernando II*, p. 221; Enríquez, *Crónica*, pp. 134–37.

40. Enríquez, *Crónica*, pp. 137–38; Suárez, "Los Trastámaras," p. 259; Vicens, *Fernando II*, pp. 222–23.

did they cost you much to rear. Know that this matter has to be handled in another way. . . .[41]

Thus, to the disgust of his followers, the king entered into negotiations. Warily, the two sides, heavily armed, agreed to meet between the towns of Cabezón and Cigales on a treeless plain to avoid the possibility of ambush. Pacheco's policy now was to rid the Consejo of the Mendozas, have Alfonso declared heir, and reorder the monarchy to make the king a pawn in noble hands. At the meeting on 25 October 1464, the terms of an agreement were reached, to be ratified later. Alfonso was to be named heir and given the mastership of Santiago and several castles for his support, but this was conditional on his marriage with Juana. Significantly, nothing was said then of the princess's supposed illegitimacy. Beltrán was to exile himself from the court for a period of six months; he duly renounced the mastership of Santiago on 29 October. Enrique compensated Beltrán by making him duke of Alburquerque and giving him the strategic towns of Roa, Aranda, Molina, Cuéllar, and Atienza. The two sides agreed to meet again at the same place in November, and Enrique used the time to bring Alfonso from Segovia.[42]

The second meeting lasted from the twentieth of November to the fifth of December. The nobles present formally ratified Alfonso as prince of Asturias and placed him in Pacheco's custody. A commission was established for the purpose of altering the structure of the kingdom's government. The king appointed two members, Pedro de Velasco and Gonzalo de Saavedra, and the nobles chose Pacheco and the count of Plasencia. Alonso de Oropesa, prior general of the order of St. Jerome, was to be the presiding member and occupy a position of neutrality. The commission was to convene later at Medina del Campo to work out the details of the reorganization. By now rumors were circulating that Juana was not the king's daughter, and Enrique was working hard to maintain his daughter's position; he repeated that Alfonso must marry no other and he brought forth medical evidence of his potency.[43]

On the last day of the meeting the nobles put out a long document which stated their demands in complete detail. The Muslims and Jews in

41. Enríquez, *Crónica*, pp. 138–39.

42. Enríquez, *Crónica*, pp. 139–40; Vicens, *Fernando II*, pp. 222–24; Suárez, "Los Trastámaras," p. 260. AGS, *Patronato Real*, *leg*. 7, fol. 111; *Colección diplomática*, docs. 100–101, 103; RAH, *Salazar*, *leg*. D-14, fols. 108–109, *leg*. F-4, fols. 119–20, *leg*. M-12, fols. 119–20.

43. Suárez, "Los Trastámaras," p. 260; *Colección diplomática*, doc. 104; Galíndez, *Crónica*, pp. 226–27.

the king's employ should be driven from the realm and their confiscated property used to ransom Christians in Muslim hands. The nobles asserted that there were heretical Christians in the land and the king "should order that great favor and help should be given to the prelates, ecclesiastical judges, and *inquisitors of heresy* in order that those who fall into error and are suspected of depraved heresy should be liberally punished and imprisoned."[44] Royal judges and officials should be accountable to the law, and the clergy should be allowed to do its work unimpeded. Financial affairs should be put in order. There had always been requests for specific reforms, but now the nobles demanded what amounted to a constitutional revolution. They stated that the Consejo should be reformed and prelates, *caballeros*, and *letrados* appointed to it. It was to be divided into two groups alternating each six months, with the ability and right to take part in all decisions of the realm. And—a very important point—those brought up for justice should be judged by their peers. What this really meant was that the rebel nobles wanted to preclude the possibility of their being judged by the new men of lower estate with whom Enrique had surrounded himself. The revolutionary clauses were carefully sandwiched among others which would elicit greater response in the lower classes, such as investigation of malpractice in the market of Medina del Campo and elsewhere and better policing of the forests of Madrid and Segovia.[45] This was the first full statement of the program the rebels followed. It was designed to establish them as the arbiters of the realm and its provisions reappear consistently in their manifestos throughout the next years.

The commission established at Cabezón-Cigales duly met in Medina del Campo, but by then Enrique's appointees had gone over to the rebel side. Ably guided by Pacheco, the commissioners published a document known as the Sentence of Medina del Campo on 16 January 1465. They had been charged with the reformation of royal government, but the statement they published, if it had been put into force, would have established and codified an oligarchy. The Sentence of Medina del Campo repeated the substance of the document of the previous month: the church was to be respected, Muslims and Jews were to be removed from the court, and an inquisition was to be established. There were provisions designed to appeal to the cities as well, such as free elections to the Cortes and no taxation imposed without the assent of the Cortes. There was to be an inquiry into the practices of royal officials, and offices were not to be

44. *Codoin,* 14:372, author's italics.
45. Ibid., 14:369–95.

inherited (it is doubtful if the nobles ever intended to implement this provision). The nobles expanded on the clause demanding a trial by one's peers. The Sentence called for a committee composed of Pacheco, Carrillo, the counts of Haro and Plasencia, two additional prelates, and the procurators of Toledo, Seville, and Burgos, without whose approval the king would be powerless to imprison a noble. To safeguard the Sentence and as a crowning blow, the standing royal army, one of Enrique's greatest achievements, was to be reduced from 3,000 to 600 *lanzas.*[46] Pacheco had pushed through a document designed to reduce the monarchy to dependence on the nobility.

Superficially, the program of the nobles as expressed seemed to show concern for the inhabitants of the towns and the desire to help them share in a well-ordered monarchical government with constitutional checks on the power of the king. Undoubtedly, baser motives were at work. The nobles called for free elections for the cities, but throughout the century they had been infiltrating the governments of the formerly independent towns and assuming control of them. To put forth the idea that offices could no longer be inherited was laudable, but would Fadrique Enríquez, for example, willingly implement the change? For decades his family had been admirals of Castile; he himself owed his office to inheritance. During the latter years of Enrique's reign there was a rising tide of opposition to Jews, Muslims, and *conversos*. The rebel leaders rode this wave with their propaganda and their proposal that an inquisition be established. The nobles really wanted a monarchy subject to their approval, one in which they would be more rulers than ruled. The leaders of the nobility, Pacheco and Carrillo especially, wanted personal power and steered the drafting of the proposals to ensure this.

Nevertheless, the Sentence of Medina del Campo did reflect the difficulties facing Castilians during the reign of Enrique IV. Nobles and urban dwellers could see in the proposals a genuine attempt to alleviate some of their greatest problems. Undoubtedly, many people endorsed the statement written by the committee. The concerns were real, and it is not fair to castigate nobles outside the rebel hierarchy for agreeing with the program of Pacheco, Carrillo, and the other committee members. Many desired reform, but they failed to understand the deviousness of its proponents.

When Enrique got word of the Sentence of Medina del Campo, he belatedly realized the dire position he occupied and finally decided to opt for war. Beltrán received the order to mobilize the royal forces. In the

46. Suárez, "Los Trastámaras," p. 262; *Colección diplomática,* doc. 109.

process, traitors were ferreted out and dismissed, among them Gonzalo de Saavedra. In February the king decreed that the Sentence of Medina del Campo was null and void and further declared that Alfonso was not to be recognized as the heir to the throne. As the royal army began to assemble at Segovia, Juana the queen, Juana the princess, and the *infanta* Isabel were given a heavy guard. Enrique secured a monetary vote from a hastily assembled rump Cortes at Salamanca. The monarch was ready for war.[47]

Then the full-scale revolt began. The noble league held Plasencia, Carrillo was in control of Avila and Medina del Campo, and Fadrique Enríquez had Valladolid and Valdenebro. All came out for Alfonso as king.

In Avila on 5 June 1465 a ceremonial dethronement of Enrique took place. Some nobles had reservations, fearing action against the king would expose them to a charge of heresy, but their leaders argued that the subjects had the right to remove an unjust king. Accordingly, they began preparations in a square near the cathedral. On a platform they placed a seated statue representing the king, provided with the royal symbols. The leaders assembled and spokesmen read a long list of grievances against Enrique, including a catalogue of his supposed vices and defects. After this, Carrillo mounted the steps and lifted off the crown, saying that Enrique was unworthy of the royal dignity. Pacheco then took away the scepter, signifying that the king had been deprived of the administration of justice. To indicate that Enrique was no longer the defender of the realm, Alvaro de Stúñiga, the count of Plasencia, extracted the sword. Other nobles removed other adornments, and, to indicate dethronement, the counts of Benavente and Paredes kicked the statue out of the chair and onto the ground. Then they ceremonially crowned Alfonso.[48] There were two kings in the land.

47. Suárez, "Los Trastámaras," pp. 262–67; Enríquez, *Crónica*, pp. 141–42. In April the king ordered Pacheco's vassals to resist the marquis, Torres Fontes, *Itinerario*, pp. 174–75.

48. There are many descriptions of the "farce of Avila." I have followed Palencia, *Crónica*, 1:167–68. The famous phrase "a tierra, puto," does not appear in Palencia, who would never have let such a juicy item pass. Valera, writing some twenty years later, must have invented it or repeated a later accretion to the traditional story: Diego de Valera, *Memorial de diversas hazañas*, ed. Juan de Mata Carriazo, Colección de crónicas españoles, no. 4 (Madrid, 1941), pp. 99. J. Lucas-Dubreton, in *El rey huraño: Enrique IV de Castilla y su época*, pp. 135–46, stated that the dethronement was much more than a mere ceremony for propagandistic purposes. The belief in magic was strong in Castile, and a leading practitioner was Alfonso Carrillo. He and others may have believed that the statue magically became the king and that the mock dethronement was an actual one.

VI

QUESTIONS OF ORTHODOXY: RELIGIOUS AND PHYSIOLOGICAL

Two important features of the rebel campaign against Enrique IV were the insistence that the king was suspect in his religion and that he could not legally claim Juana as his daughter and heir. We can disprove the first assertion. The second takes us into the nebulous region of the sexual and physiological conditions of the king. Our task here is complicated. Enrique was a reticent man and almost all the available evidence comes from his enemies. At a remove of five centuries, we can never hope for definite answers, but we can show that in this case ultimate truth is secondary and that for contemporaries the question was decided on legal and political grounds.

First we must deal with religious matters. Both in their manifestos before the dethronement and in subsequent letters to the pope justifying their position, the rebels accused Enrique IV of lax Christianity, failure to prosecute the Granadan War, and excessive favor for Muslims, Jews, and *conversos*. I am convinced that this was nothing more than propaganda, a contrived ideological justification for rebellion. This is not to deny that religious tensions were present and increasing in Castile during Enrique's reign, but with one exception—his tactics against Granada—Enrique's policies were identical to those of Fernando and Isabel. To demonstrate this assertion, it is necessary to examine the problems of the religious groups and Christian orthodoxy and Enrique's attitudes and actions.

For centuries Jews had enjoyed more toleration in Iberia than in any other part of Christian Europe. The crisis for the Jews of the Christian kingdoms began in the middle decades of the fourteenth century. After the Black Death of 1348-50, the Christian populace began to heed sermons accusing the Jews of perfidy and to see the Jews as instigators of the hardships accompanying the Black Death. The urban revolts of the 1390s are well known and well documented, but recently Philippe Wolff has called into question their predominantly anti-Semitic character. His conclusion—with qualifications—is that social and economic tensions were probably the primary motivations, while religious hostility was secondary.[1] But forced conversions accompanied the revolts, and in the last decade of the fourteenth century and the first decade of the fifteenth, there developed a new social group—the *conversos.*[2] Most conversions had been undertaken in a period of intense fear and mob hysteria. Leaving aside any religious connotation, on one level there were advantages to be gained by the new converts. They were now free from social or legal restrictions and ostensibly could enter into Christian society freely.

Despite their apparent freedom the *conversos* were in an impossible situation. Jews who had remained faithful denounced them. Many Christians refused to accept them as true equals. *Conversos* who had accepted baptism in a fit of panic found themselves trapped. If they sincerely tried to follow the new religion they were still suspect, often simply because they could not assimilate Christian customs overnight, and if they tried to carry on their old religion secretly while outwardly conforming to Christianity, they could be denounced to ecclesiastical courts. In addition they continued in one of the most visible occupations of the Jews in Christian Spain—that of tax collector. As a result they were exposed to the hatred of taxpayers, all those who did not have noble or clerical status. Members of the lower classes learned to hate the person who collected taxes, and if that person was a *converso*, the hatred was doubled. In fifteenth-century France, urban unrest had a direct relation to increases in taxation, and

1. Philippe Wolff, "The 1391 Pogrom in Spain: Social Crisis or Not?" *Past and Present* 50 (February 1971):4–18. For the impact of the Black Death on Jewish-Christian relations, see José Amador de los Ríos, *Historia social, política, y religiosa de los Judíos de España,* 2 (Madrid, 1875), pp. 257–61. For the Trastámara revolution and its religious overtones: Yitzhak Baer, *A History of the Jews in Christian Spain,* 2 (Philadelphia, 1961); Salo Wittmayer Baron, *A Social and Religious History of the Jews,* 9 (Philadelphia, New York, and London, 1967), pp. 232–34; Julio Valdeón Baruque, *Los Judíos de Castilla y la revolución Trastámara* (Valladolid, 1969); and idem, *Enrique II de Castilla: La guerra civil y la consolidación del régimen (1366–1371)* (Valladolid, 1966).
2. For the *conversos,* see the works of three specialists: the two important works of Francisco Márques Villanueva, "Conversos y cargos concejiles en el siglo XV," *Revista de Archivos, Bibliotecas, y Museos* 63 (1957):503–540, and "The Converso Problem: An Assessment," in *Collected Studies in Honour of Américo Castro's Eightieth Year,* ed. M.P. Hornik (Oxford, 1965), pp. 317–33; see also Haim Beinart, "The Converso Community in 15th Century Spain," in *The Sephardi Heritage: Essays in the History and Cultural Contribution of the Jews of Spain and Portugal,* ed. R.D. Barnett, vol. 1 (London, 1971), pp. 425–56; and the numerous studies by Américo Castro, particularly *The Spaniards: An Introduction to Their History,* trans. W.F. King and S. Margaretten (Berkeley, Los Angeles, and London, 1971).

there the collectors were indistinguishable from the taxpayers. It is easy to imagine how much worse it must have been in the peninsula.

So the *conversos* were truly trapped. The church did not sanction forced baptisms, but if they occurred, it considered them binding. The *conversos* could not return to Judaism; if they did, they would be punished for apostasy. Nor were the sincere converts fully accepted in their new faith. As if to cap matters, some of the *conversos*—perhaps insecure in their new status and hopeful of buttressing their own positions—became the most fanatical accusers of both Jews and *conversos*. In such circumstances it is not surprising that demands arose for an inquisition to examine suspected cases of *converso* wrongdoing. An insidious process was at work: whereas before anti-Jewish feeling was based on religion, and a Jew could escape by conversion, by the late fifteenth century the intolerance was based on ethnic grounds, from which there was no escape.[3]

During the reign of Juan II, the relations between Christians and Jews regained some degree of the former toleration and there was a respite from hostility. Restrictions against the Jews were generally relaxed and in some cases abolished. The Jews had suffered greatly; their numbers were reduced by mass conversions. While it is extremely difficult to estimate the numbers and percentages of Jews and *conversos*, it is clear that the pressure and mass conversions had particularly affected the wealthiest and most prominent individuals and the most flourishing Jewish communities in the largest cities. The Jews in the smaller towns were less affected, and throughout the fifteenth century they continued their accustomed occupations as shopkeepers, physicians, tax farmers, and financial agents.[4]

After the wave of violence receded, there were still unconverted Jews in Castile, and the Christian impetus to insist on their conversion, although less violent, was no less persistent. Along with the *conversos*, the Jews suffered the hostility of the Christian populace. The lower classes demonstrated particular hatred, projecting their feelings of impotence on the Jews, possibly encouraged in this by members of the nobility.[5]

The first significant outbreak of popular hysteria in the fifteenth century occurred in Toledo in 1449. It is difficult to assign a priority of

3. Henry Charles Lea, *A History of the Inquisition of Spain*, 1 (New York, 1906), p. 126.
4. Baer, *Jews in Christian Spain*, 1:190–91; Angus McKay, "Popular Movements and Pogroms in Fifteenth-Century Castile," *Past and Present* 55 (May 1972):33–67, especially 38–39.
5. Julio Caro Baroja, *Los Judíos en la España moderna y contemporánea*, 1 (Madrid, 1961), pp. 96–97.

causes; the background was complex, involving political, economic, and religious factors. One immediate cause was a widely disliked tax imposed on the kingdom by Alvaro de Luna, the favorite of Juan II and *de facto* ruler of Castile. A portion of the nobility disliked his power and the consequent strengthening of the authority of the king. To add to the difficulty, two *conversos*, Alonso de Cota and Juan de la Ciudad, had charge of collecting the tax in Toledo. Under the leadership of Pedro Sarmiento, Toledo's Old Christians rose and first attacked the houses of the tax collectors before turning to a general assault on the entire Jewish quarter. After much bloodshed, order returned and Sarmiento fled the city. But in the course of the uprising, local clerics tried and punished *conversos* for anti-Christian acts and attitudes. More ominously, Sarmiento issued a notorious *Sententia-estatuto*, probably drafted by Marcos García de Mazarambros, supposedly repeating anti-Semitic Castilian laws promulgated in the 1390s, but in fact extending to *conversos* provisions previously applicable only to Jews. By the terms of the edict, all *conversos* were forever excluded from any public office, civil or ecclesiastical, which would give them authority over Old Christians, and in addition they could no longer act as notaries or witnesses. The events in Toledo had their parallel in similar action in Ciudad Real. Even though the Castilian government refused recognition of the *Sententia-estatuto* and Pope Nicholas V annulled it, similar attempts to restrict the activities of New Christians remained alive.[6]

During the reign of Enrique IV and especially in the later years, a series of battles between Old and New Christians broke out in many Castilian cities. Violent demonstrations were especially prevalent in the south—Jaén, Córdoba, and Seville—but they also occurred in such places as Toledo. The usual pattern was for some small spark to ignite latent unrest, and after a period of fighting the victorious Old Christians either forced the Jews and *conversos* from the city or excluded them from public office.[7] Those who remained had to live in ghettos (*aljamas*) and wear distinctive dress.

6. Fernán Pérez de Guzmán, *La crónica del serenísimo príncipe Don Juan, segundo rey deste nombre en Castilla y en León*, ed. Cayetano Rosell, in *Biblioteca de autores españoles* 68 (Madrid, 1953), p. 664; Eloy Benito Ruano, *Toledo en el siglo XV: Vida política* (Madrid, 1961), pp. 38–58; Baer, *Jews in Christian Spain*, 2:277–82; Caro Baroja, *Los Judíos*, 1:123–28. Pope Nicholas V in his bull *Humani generis* (24 December 1449) annulled the anti-*converso* decrees: Archivo Vaticano, Reg. Vat., vol. 410, fols. 130–32, printed by V. Beltrán de Heredía, "Las bulas de Nicolás V acerca de los conversos de Castilla," *Sefarad* 21 (1961):41–44.

7. The events of Córdoba are described in Lorenzo Galíndez de Carvajal, *Crónica de Enrique IV*, in Juan Torres Fontes, *Estudio sobre la "Crónica de Enrique IV" del Dr. Galíndez de Carvajal* (Murcia, 1946), pp. 448–50.

The example of Córdoba in 1474 will serve to illustrate the general course of events. There was an underlying bitterness on the part of the Old Christians in Córdoba, due mainly to the wealth of the New Christians and their offices in the municipal government. One day a procession of the Cofradía de la Caridad (which excluded *conversos*) wound through the streets carrying a statue of the Virgin. As the parade passed the house of a *converso*, a servant—a child less than ten years old—threw a bucket of water or urine from a second floor window, which happened to hit the Virgin's statue. The outcome was a three-day battle in which the houses of many *conversos* were burned. The *conversos* responded by burning the residences of Old Christians. Each side perpetrated robberies, murders, and rapes on the other. In consequence, the *conversos* were banned from holding public offices in the city.[8] Similar events in other cities followed roughly the same course.

But the riots in the cities were local affairs with little if any impact on the politics of the kingdom as a whole. When more local studies are available, we may be able to trace common threads, but for now it is sufficient to note that the factions contesting for the crown did not differ in their religious policies. Henry Kamen has suggested a Marxist model to encompass both rising hostility to non-Christians and a supposed noble move to control the economy. In his view the greatest noble fear was a challenge to their economic supremacy. This challenge he identified with a rising bourgeoisie, whose most vigorous members were Jews and *conversos*. The noble attack reached its culmination with the establishment of the Inquisition directed against the *conversos* and the expulsion of the Jews who would not convert. The nobles found their views and their economic position ratified by the *Reyes Católicos* and were thus able to keep Spain economically and intellectually backward until the coming of industrial capitalism in the nineteenth century.[9]

Kamen's model is incomplete and it distorts certain factors to make them fit neatly therein. He gives the bourgeoisie a far more significant role than it deserves; the very word *burguesía* had almost completely fallen into disuse in the fifteenth century because there was no class corresponding to the term. We know that the nobles were greatly divided on almost every score. Certain nobles argued strongly against the establishment of the Inquisition and the expulsion of the Jews. The only consistency of the nobles was in their desire to enhance their own power and their control of revenue-

8. Ibid.; Caro Baroja, *Los Judíos*, 1:131–34.
9. Henry Kamen, *The Spanish Inquisition* (New York, 1968).

producing offices and holdings, but their targets were primarily other nobles or the crown. While we can reject the assertion that the nobles consistently acted as a class, we simply do not have enough local studies to be sure of the applicability of sweeping generalizations about the actions of the aristocracy regarding Jews and *conversos* or the responses of the lower classes.

In the main Enrique followed past practice in his treatment of the religious minorities. He continually employed Jews; four were court physicians and one, Levi Acuña, was a king's judge.[10] Many Jews were tax farmers, but since they were not on the royal payroll, their names have mainly been forgotten. Enrique rewarded Abraham Abenzayd, Rabbi Jacob Aben Núñez, and Isaque Abenzahal Zafer for their unspecified "buenos servicios."[11] But he was not loath to issue decrees against Jews and *conversos*. In 1460 he ordered that the Jews of Murcia could own neither horses nor arms.[12] In July 1468 he deprived the *conversos* of Toledo of the positions they held as city councilmen.[13]

His most interesting anticipation of Fernando and Isabel's policies was the establishment in 1462, at the urging of Alfonso de Oropesa, prior general of the order of Saint Jerome, of an inquisition, the first ever in Castile and different from the medieval papal inquisition because of the crown's proposal to appoint the inquisitors. Enrique's actions seem to suggest that he was concerned over the violence between the Old and New Christians and hoped to calm the situation by disproving most of the charges against the *conversos*. One story amply demonstrates Enrique's attitude. A vehemently anti-Semitic Franciscan, Fernando de la Plaza, in the course of a sermon preached at court stated that he could produce the foreskins of the sons of highly placed *conversos*. The king was annoyed. He insisted that the friar prove his assertions and name the *conversos* responsible. De la Plaza proved unable to do so, and Oropesa decided to preach several sermons against such dangerous libels.[14] The records are very sparse, but

10. AGS, *Quitaciones de Corte, legs*. 2–4.
11. AGS, *Mercedes y privilegios, leg*. 34, fols. 20, 22, 25.
12. Juan Torres Fontes, *Intinerario de Enrique IV de Castilla* (Murcia, 1955), p. 106.
13. *Colección diplomática*, doc. 147.
14. Diego Enríquez del Castillo, *Crónica del rey Don Enrique el cuarto de este nombre*, ed. Cayetano Rosell, in *Biblioteca de autores españoles* 70 (Madrid, (1953), p. 130; Tarsicio de Azcona, *Isabel de Castilla: Estudio crítico sobre su vida y su reinado* (Madrid, 1964), pp. 377–82; Caro Baroja, *Los Judíos*, 1:138–39; Baer, *Jews in Christian Spain*, 2:288–90. Enrique's request for an inquisition is found in the Archivo Vaticano, Reg. Suppl. 547, fols. 188–89, and is printed in V. Beltrán de Heredía, "Las bulas," pp. 44–45.

certain evidence exists that the first Castilian inquisition was ineffective, or at least unsatisfying for an important group of the high nobility. We have already examined the Sentence of Medina del Campo set forth in late 1464 and early 1465—over two years after the inquisition was proposed. In it the nobles called for the appointment of "inquisitors of heresy in order that those who fall into error and are suspected of depraved heresy should be liberally punished and imprisoned."[15] Since the king rejected the entire Sentence and a rebellion ensued, the full inquisition had to await the accession of Isabel.

The other religious minority, the Mudéjares, occupied a different position. They were few in number and scattered over the southern half of the kingdom. They were neither politically nor socially as prominent as the Jews and *conversos*. Since wealthy and powerful Muslims had retreated southward to Granada and North Africa as the reconquest advanced, those who remained tended to occupy humble positions as farmers and artisans. Less prosperous and less visible, they were insulated from the hostility of the Christian masses. Only some four percent of the Castilian population in the fifteenth century, they were not a significant factor in Castilian society until their numbers leaped with the conquest of Granada.

As was the case in his attitude toward Jews and *conversos*, Enrique IV felt no irrational hatred toward the Muslims, either those in Castile or in Granada. In this he squarely occupied the ground laid out by the men of the medieval reconquest. To Spanish leaders from El Cid onward, the Muslims were not implacable enemies to be met only with fire and sword. They were men whose lands could be conquered when convenient but who could serve equally as allies and trading partners at other times. Castilian kings had never felt the need for an all-out onslaught against the Muslims, and Enrique obviously shared this view. His belief was the basis for the successful if unspectacular policy he followed toward Granada.

In his entourage Enrique employed a guard unit consisting of *guardas moriscos* and *caballeros moriscos*, a legacy from his father. In fact Juan II employed many more *moriscos* than did Enrique. This "moorish" guard has been used continually as part of an indictment of Enrique as a lax Christian and as one secretly inclined to Islam. Nothing could be farther from the truth. The guards were all converts to Christianity, and in certain cases the employment records conserved in the archive of Simancas indicate that the guards owed their positions and salaries to the fact of their

15. *Codoin*, 14:372.

conversion.[16] There was an incident between the *guardas moriscos* and the people of Segovia, after which Enrique sent the *moriscos* to Madrid, but there is no evidence that the disturbance was caused by religious animosity.[17]

We are fortunate in having the records of two groups of foreign travelers who visited Castile in Enrique's time. Both accounts provide pertinent information about the ambience of the royal court. As is the case with the available chronicles of the reign, most historians have relied on the harsher contemporary account, in this case that of those who accompanied Leo of Rozmital. In 1465 Rozmital and a suite of some forty followers undertook a tour of the courts of western Europe at the behest of the Bohemian king, George Podêbrad. *The Travels of Leo of Rozmital* consists of a parallel set of narratives, one by Gabriel Tetzel and the other by a squire known as Schaseck. As they passed through Castile in 1466 or 1467, Rozmital and his group were awed by viewing Enrique's treasury in the *alcázar* of Segovia, but the king himself left a worse impression. After being exposed to the poor accommodations for travelers in Castile, then in the midst of a civil war, a small number of the group met Enrique, who was "sitting on the floor on carpets in the heathen manner," and made arrangements for Rozmital to meet the king at Olmedo. In Tetzel's words:

> As the King was not there, the knight conducted my lord into the King's apartment which is splendidly built where the King had a stately meal to be prepared. . . . Then the knight conducted my lord to a little town . . . where we found the King. We were lodged in a wretched inn with only two rooms on the naked earth, and we had to leave our horses outside the town. The inhabitants are for the most part heathens. The old King has many at his court and has driven out many Christians and given their land to the heathen. Also he eats and drinks and is clothed in the heathen manner and is an enemy of Christians. He has committed a great crime and follows unchristian ways.[18]

At first reading this seems to confirm the unfavorable interpretations of Enrique IV. But there are problems and internal contradictions in Tetzel's account. On the very page after he described Enrique's gracious treatment of them, Tetzel complained that the king "showed my lord no

16. AGS, *Quitaciones de Corte, legs.* 1–4. I found 78 *moriscos* appointed by Juan II, and while Enrique IV kept some of his father's appointees on the salary rolls, he appointed only ten new *moriscos.*

17. Galíndez, *Crónica*, pp. 262–63.

18. *The Travels of Leo of Rozmital*, trans. and ed. Malcolm Letts, Hakluyt Society Publications, 2nd series, no. 108 (Cambridge, 1957), pp. 91–92.

honour. . . ."[19] It is probable that he heard and was convinced by the rebel polemics, especially since he gave a lengthy and generally accurate account of the dethronement at Avila, which had occurred at least two years previously.[20] It is likely that Tetzel could not distinguish between Castilian Christians and non-Christians. The "heathens" he mentioned as attacking the party were specifically identified as Christians by Tetzel's companion Schaseck,[21] who also reported that in the same town there were "many heathen called Saracens, but which are the better men? I should not find it easy to decide."[22] A possible source of the hostile attitude of Tetzel might have been the court of Juan II of Aragon, where Rozmital's party spent several pleasant days.[23]

There is another account of a Castilian visit by a central European: *The Diary of Jörg von Ehingen*, a knight of a prominent Swabian family. He took up the life of a soldier of fortune, and after visiting the Holy Land and later fighting with the Portuguese at Ceuta, he came to Castile in about 1457 or 1458 to participate in one of Enrique's Granadan campaigns. After its conclusion Ehingen spent two months of recuperation in the Castilian court. He had nothing at all unusual to report about the Castilian king or his followers, mentioning only "feasting, dancing, hunting, horse-racing, and such-like pastimes," and specifically calling Enrique the "Christian King."[24]

Ehingen had been in many Christian and Muslim lands, and so it is more remarkable that he made no comment about Islamic-like practices in Castile. Possibly he recognized that most border societies adopt some of the superficial customs of those on the other side of the frontier. Tetzel, since Castile was the first country in real contact with Islam that he visited, was overly impressed by the unusual features of Castilian society to the extent that he could mistake Christians for "heathens."

Historians have often followed the account of Tetzel and denounced the Islamic-influenced customs of the Castilian court in cuisine, dress, and furnishings. Claudio Sánchez-Albornoz even wrote of the "maurofilia" of Enrique IV.[25] But on the whole Enrique's practices do not seem greatly

19. Ibid., p. 93.
20. Ibid., pp. 127–28.
21. Ibid., pp. 95–96.
22. Ibid., p. 96.
23. Ibid., pp. 132–33, 135–36.
24. Jörg von Ehingen, *The Diary of Jörg von Ehingen*, trans. and ed. Malcolm Letts (London, 1929), pp. 38–39.
25. Claudio Sánchez-Albornoz, *España: Un enigma histórico*, 1 (Buenos Aires, 1962), pp. 664–65.

unlike those of his predecessors or successors. Spaniards of all classes had been influenced by the Muslim style of life. Domestic arrangements as late as the seventeenth century were as akin to Muslim as to European patterns. We can still see one example in the home of Cervantes's father in Alcalá de Henares. In the late sixteenth century a principal room on the ground floor was furnished with low divans for the segregated relaxation of the women of the house—a Christian adaptation of the Islamic *harim*. There is a study of the wardrobe of Isabel *la Católica* showing that many of her clothes and accessories, while entirely acceptable and fashionable in Castile, were in the Muslim style, some even decorated with Arabic script.[26]

While Enrique's toleration and some of his tastes were completely in keeping with the practice of his medieval predecessors, his attitudes toward Muslims, Jews, and *conversos* cannot be used to brand the king as a bad Christian. He was conventionally pious, and his distaste for bloodshed indicates that he was much closer to the tenets of Christianity than some of the leading churchmen of the day. Galíndez de Carvajal, whose chronicle was commissioned by Isabel, reported that Enrique was very religious and kept the divine offices well.[27] His recorded speeches include the usual expressions of Christian belief. Like all good medieval kings, he founded monasteries; two in Segovia—Santa María del Parral and San Antonio—and San Jerónimo del Paso in Madrid. He made some twenty-five grants to religious institutions for repairs and new buildings, and bestowed privileges on them, such as permission to hold markets.

So the image becomes clear of a king who was a good Christian but who was swayed by the forces of the day. We must conclude that Enrique hardly differed from his successors in religious policies. Accusations to the contrary were politically motivated.

But what about Juana, and her right to the throne? Was she truly Enrique's daughter? Here the issues and the evidence are far less clear, and conclusions will probably always be tentative. The passage of time and the demise of documents have rendered certainty elusive if not impossible. With the reliability of contemporary records skewed by partisan polemics, it is difficult to reach a satisfying resolution of the baffling sexual history of Enrique IV.

Gregorio Marañón some forty years ago suggested that while still capable of generation, Enrique was a homosexual.[28] This interpretation

26. Carmen Bernis, "Modas moriscas en la sociedad cristiana del siglo XV y principios del XVI," *Boletín de la Real Academia de la Historia* 144 (1959):199–228.

27. Galíndez, *Crónica*, p. 75.

28. Gregorio Marañón, *Ensayo biológico sobre Enrique IV de Castilla y su tiempo*, 10th ed. (Madrid, 1964), especially pp. 98-108.

needs careful consideration. Much of Marañón's evidence comes from the bitterly biased chronicle of Alonso de Palencia, whose hatred of Enrique led him to make many questionable assertions, most of which can be successfully countered and discounted. But the idea of homosexuality must still be entertained. Pulgar gave an enigmatic glimpse of Enrique's early years when he stated that:

> During [his youth] he gave himself some delights which youth demands to be satisfied and honesty calls to be denied. They became a habit because . . . weak youth [did not] know how to refrain. . . .[29]

Another chronicler—Pedro Carrillo de Huete—reported that while Enrique was still prince he developed a great affection for Rodrigo Portocarrero. Pacheco and Girón had to go to great lengths to reduce Portocarrero's influence over Enrique.[30]

Enrique's lifelong relations with Pacheco suggest the possibility of a homosexual bond. They had been companions since youth, and Enrique consistently forgave Pacheco's betrayals and brought him back into the circle of royal advisers when his actions had been unforgivable. But again the sources are so ambiguous that we can never be really sure. Perhaps there was a homosexual attraction between them that Pacheco exploited, perhaps they openly indulged in homosexual relations, perhaps the feelings were covert or subconscious in both parties. Part of the rebel disaffection toward the king could be explained on the basis of the mere suspicion of such a relation. Machiavelli would soon write that "a prince will be despised if he is considered . . . effeminate . . . and he should guard himself against such a reputation as against a most dangerous reef."[31] Even if such was not true in Enrique's case, his enemies could use the imputation as an effective tool against him.

Enrique's long marriage to Blanca de Navarra was fruitless; the union was never consummated. The initial failure could be ascribed to the youth of the monarch and the semi-public nature of the royal act of love, possibly with the additional impediment of the prince's affection for Pacheco if it existed. The sources are reasonably clear that nothing took place between prince and princess, and that Blanca was a virgin when Enrique divorced her. The second marriage to Juana of Portugal is more puzzling. The chronicles indicate a failure to consummate the marriage on the wedding night,

29. Fernando del Pulgar, *Claros varones de Castilla*, ed. R.B. Tate (Oxford, 1971), p. 5.
30. Pedro Carrillo de Huete, *Crónica del halconero de Juan II*, ed. Juan de Mata Carriazo, Colección de crónicas españoles, no. 8 (Madrid, 1946), pp. 540, 543.
31. Niccolò Machiavelli, *The Prince*, trans. and ed. T.G. Bergin (New York, 1947), p. 53.

but it is likely that it was consummated later. Juana had a daughter after some seven years of marriage, and shortly afterwards she delivered a stillborn male fetus of six months.[32] That Enrique believed these were his children is beyond dispute. He portrayed and believed himself to be potent. At his divorce proceedings from Blanca, Segovian women had testified to his virility, and to the scandal of the court he even had an affair with Doña Guiomar, one of the highborn Portuguese ladies who had come to Castile in the court of his second wife.[33] Marañón believed that Enrique was in fact capable of generation, but that his potency was weak and intermittent.[34]

Daniel Eisenberg has recently delivered a devastating attack on Marañón's interpretations, demolishing Marañón's diagnosis of acromegalic eunuchoidism, an endocrine imbalance resulting in a combination of acromegaly—the adult form characterized by abnormal growth in the peripheral areas of the skull, jaws, hands, and feet—and eunuchoidism—characterized by the appearance of feminine characteristics in the adult male. For Marañón, this endocrine imbalance caused homosexuality. Eisenberg notes that the medical profession has long discarded any belief in a physiological basis of homosexuality, and he dismisses eunuchoidism on the sensible grounds that all chroniclers agree that the bearded Enrique exhibited masculine features.[35] This leaves him with acromegaly.

To diagnose acromegaly in Enrique IV, Eisenberg uses the chronicler Enríquez's description of the king. Cited in full it says:

> He was a person of tall stature and heavy in the body, and of strong limbs; he had large and strong (*recios*) fingers; the appearance was fierce, almost like a lion, the view of which struck terror to those who saw him; the nose very Roman and wide, not that he was born this

32. Azcona, *Isabel*, pp. 40–42. On p. 38 Azcona demonstrates that seven years before a first pregnancy was not unusual among the royalty of the period.
33. Enríquez, *Crónica*, p. 112; Alonso de Palencia, *Crónica de Enrique IV*, trans. Antonio Paz y Meliá, 2 vols., in *Biblioteca de autores españoles* 207–208 (Madrid, 1973–1975), 1:83.
34. Marañón, *Ensayo biológico*, pp. 63–67. Marañón first put forth his ideas in "Ensayo biológico sobre Enrique IV de Castilla," *Boletín de la Real Academia de la Historia* 96 (1930):11–93. His conclusions were most succinctly stated there: "all these complexities do not invalidate the absolute possibility that [Enrique] was capable of isolated and effective sexual relations with his second wife . . . nor that . . . he could have been the father of La Beltraneja. . . . Biologically and historically . . . there is no reason that should contradict the legitimacy of Doña Juana, the so-called Beltraneja" (p. 93).
35. Daniel Eisenberg, "Enrique IV and Gregorio Marañón," *Renaissance Quarterly* 29 (1976):21–29.

> way, but because in his youth he received an injury there; blue, somewhat widely set eyes, the eyelids reddish. . . . The head large and round; the face wide; the eyebrows high; the temples sunken; the jaws long and stretched at the lower part; the teeth thick and close (*traspellados*); blond hair; the beard long and not often shaved; the complexion of the face between ruddy and dark; the skin very white; the legs very long and well sculpted; the feet delicate.[36]

Eisenberg feels this description suggests the presence of acromegaly. "The group of symptoms, once pointed out, is easy to recognize. The large, thick fingers, the lion-like appearance . . . , the oversized skull with its protruding jaw and misplaced teeth, the enlarged barrel chest. . . ."[37] I think Eisenberg was overly zealous in his attempted diagnosis. The difference is the degree of emphasis and the alternate translations of adjectives. The king's head may only have been large, not oversized; the protruding jaw may only have been prominent; the large, thick fingers may only have been large and strong; the teeth, closely set, not misplaced. If acromegaly were present, the feet, too, would have shown abnormality, but Enríquez calls them delicate.

Since Enríquez was the court chronicler, it would be well to examine Palencia's description of the king. Palencia was hostile and constantly uttered libellous statements against Enrique, but his portrait agrees closely with that of Enríquez.

> . . . the deformed nose, squashed, broken in the middle as a consequence of a fall in youth, gave him a great resemblance to a monkey; his thin lips gave no grace to the mouth; the wide cheek bones made the face ugly, and the beard, long and protruding, made the profile of the face seem concave, as if something were missing in the center. The rest of the person was of a perfectly formed man.[38]

Although these descriptions do not support Eisenberg, the disease is a progressive one—as he informs us—and these two portraits come from early periods of Enrique's life, Palencia's while he was still prince, Enríquez's at the time of his coronation. Perhaps the physical symptoms increased later in the king's life, but the chroniclers do not mention them. Eisenberg goes on to note that several emotional reactions of the king resemble those experienced by victims of acromegaly.

36. Enríquez, *Crónica*, pp. 100-101.
37. Eisenberg, "Enrique IV and Gregorio Marañón," p. 26.
38. Palencia, *Crónica*, 1:11.

Another physical manifestation of acromegaly is the enlargement of the genitals. And here we have a famous description by the German Münzer who traveled in Spain in 1494 and 1495. He said that Enrique's penis was small near the base and large at the end, so that penetration was not possible. According to Münzer, Enrique's semen was watery and sterile.[39] Eisenberg uses this story—characterized as a bordello tale by the translator, who chose to leave it in Latin—as additional evidence for acromegaly. Possibly, but the story came to Münzer at the court of the Catholic Monarchs, twenty years after Isabel had assumed the crown of Castile in questionable legal circumstances and whose advocates, such as Palencia, would go to any lengths to discredit her half brother.

Finally, we have the evidence of the king's remains, exhumed from their resting place in the monastery of Guadalupe in 1946 by Marañón and the archeologist Manuel Gómez Moreno. According to their findings, the skeleton of the king measured 1.7 meters, indicating a height in life of about 1.8 meters, or just over five feet, nine inches. The chest with the largest diameter of fifty centimeters was "equal to that of any robust living man." The legs were long in relation to the trunk, "no detail could be noted respecting the arms . . . nor the hands, with fingers which seem strong and large, because of the destruction of time; the same is true for the feet."[40] Marañón made no mention of abnormalities, which would have been apparent if the king had suffered from acromegaly.

Thus the sexual history of Enrique IV remains elusive. Even if we could be certain, the determination would have little bearing on the case at hand. Enrique always regarded Juana as his daughter and was never swayed by claims to the contrary. At the time of her birth, the kingdom—both nobles and Cortes—accepted Juana as the king's daughter. Questions about her legitimacy only arose later and were the product of a propaganda campaign directed toward discrediting her along with her father. There were rumors, most of them ascribing responsibility for the child to Beltrán de la Cueva, but again these surfaced only later. The best case for Juana includes the following points: she was the queen's daughter, she was born in the royal household and her birth was welcomed by the king, the kingdom recognized her as the legal heir, and international opinion saw her as the king's daughter. For his part, Enrique never—not even under the pressure of the meeting at Toros de Guisando—denied her as his daughter.

39. J. Münzer, "Relación del viaje," trans. Julio Puyol, in *Viajes de extranjeros por España y Portugal*, ed. J. García Mercadal, vol. 1 (Madrid, 1952), pp. 403–404.
40. Marañón, *Ensayo biológico*, pp. 24–25.

Whether they were true or not, the accusations of religious unorthodoxy and sexual incompetence were helpful for the rebels. They also aided Isabel's later campaign for the throne, even though the accusations—on a legal plane—against Juana were based on irregularities in the use of the papal dispensation for the king's marriage, not on biological grounds.

VII

DISSENSION, DECLINE, AND DEATH

When the news spread of the ceremony of dethronement in Avila, the kingdom fell rapidly into two camps as partly concealed divisions came to the surface. The roster of insurgents included familiar names; in addition to Pacheco and Carrillo, the admiral Fadrique Enríquez and his brother Enrique came out for prince Alfonso, as did Pedro Girón, Pedro Fajardo, the Manriques, Alvaro Pérez de Guzmán, and Lope de Stúñiga. The duke of Medina Sidonia, Juan de Guzmán, and the count of Arcos, Juan Ponce de León, wrote from Seville asking money from Alfonso for the defense of that city, but they no doubt hoped more for their own gain than Alfonso's. Enrique's usual followers rallied behind the king: Beltrán de la Cueva, the marquis of Santillana (Diego Hurtado de Mendoza), Pedro González de Mendoza (as this point bishop of Calahorra), and the rest of the Mendozas along with Alvar Pérez Osorio, Miguel Lucas de Iranzo, and Juan de Valenzuela. A majority of the bishops of the kingdom fell in with the loyalist faction.[1]

Enrique quickly began to mount a counterattack. The army was divided in half, part facing the rebel forces and the rest providing an escort for the queen, who went to the Portuguese border to meet with Afonso V. Significantly, Isabel was to accompany the queen. Pacheco stealthily approached the king and said that the rising had occurred against his will and that he would work to quell the revolt. Even the trusting Enrique was skeptical.[2] To his assembled followers, Enrique stressed his divine ordination and his conviction that heavenly intervention would favor the true king and punish the rebels. He also expressed his horror of unnecessary

1. Alonso de Palencia, *Crónica de Enrique IV*, trans. Antonio Paz y Meliá, 2 vols., in *Biblioteca de autores españoles* 207–208 (Madrid, 1973-1975), 1:167–68, 171–73, gives the names of the adherents of both factions. The letter of Medina Sidonia and Arcos is in AHN, *Osuna, carpeta* 38, no. 9.

2. Diego Enríquez del Castillo, *Crónica del rey Don Enrique el cuarto de este nombre*, ed. Cayetano Rosell, in *Biblioteca de autores españoles* 70 (Madrid, 1953), pp. 149–50.

bloodshed and hoped that full and open warfare would be avoided.[3] In addition the king dictated a letter, to be circulated among the cities, in which he spelled out his views. He named the conspirators and said that the sole purpose of the coronation of the young Alfonso was to enable the leaders to run the country for their own ends. He asked for men and arms to be quickly forthcoming and promised liberal rewards for support.[4] Both sides addressed letters to the pope justifying their positions.[5]

Many nobles used the confusion to plunder on their own account, Pedro Girón as usual being among the prime offenders. Many municipalities lost their last urban privileges as the nobles asserted complete jurisdiction over them. Brigandage, always something of a problem, became endemic. The urban response was the strengthening of the *Hermandades*, now banded together to present a united front to protect the towns from anarchy. While most towns favored Enrique, the civic leaders of Seville jointly wrote to Fernando Ponce de León to come home and discuss possible aid for Alfonso.[6]

The first clash between the two armies occurred at Simancas, a fortified town not far from Valladolid, where Fadrique Enríquez had raised Alfonso's flag. Pacheco had the rebel army assemble in Valladolid and move to Simancas. Prominent among the attackers was Archbishop Carrillo, recently arrived after having taken the town of Peñaflor without a battle. Simancas resisted, and Enrique promised the townspeople large rewards if they would continue the resistance.[7] Simancas was important to the king because his own forces were still slowly forming up and he needed time to bring them to fighting pitch.

During the bloody siege, which lasted two months, the page boys in the besieged town staged a demonstration of support for Enrique IV. The whole kingdom knew of the dethronement at Avila, so the young soldiers decided to stage a parody of it. They dressed a statue in ecclesiastical garb to resemble Carrillo and named the statue Don Oppas, who was believed to be the brother of Count Julian who, according to legend, aided the

3. Ibid., pp. 150–51.
4. Enrique IV, letter to Guadalajara, 16 June 1465, quoted in Francisco Layna Serrano, *Historia de Guadalajara y sus Mendozas en los siglos XV y XVI*, 4 vols. (Madrid, 1942), 2:449–50.
5. Enrique's letter to the pope is in *Colección diplomática*, doc. 124; his instructions to his ambassadors in Rome, ibid., doc. 126.
6. AHN, *Osuna*, *carpeta* 38, no. 10.
7. Lorenzo Galíndez de Carvajal, *Crónica de Enrique IV*, in Juan Torres Fontes, *Estudio sobre la "Crónica de Enrique IV" de Dr. Galíndez de Carvajal* (Murcia, (1946), pp. 246–47.

Muslims in their first incursion into the peninsula. By implication, Carrillo was working for the downfall of Enrique's monarchy as Oppas had helped bring down that of the Visigoths. When the statue was completed, the soldiers held a mocking ceremony of abuse and then the pages dragged the statue through the streets of Simancas singing a couplet which would become famous:

Esta es Simancas, don Oppas traidor
Esta es Simancas, que no Peñaflor.[8]

The siege was long and much of Simancas was destroyed. In their zeal the besieged townspeople destroyed a section of their own town to prevent its capture. The two months of the siege was just the length of time Enrique needed, and his appreciation was boundless. He granted the inhabitants three great privileges, which they enjoyed even into the nineteenth century. All the male inhabitants and their descendants were made *hidalgos*, the city was declared independent of the jurisdiction of Valladolid, and it was exempted from payment of the *alcabala* and other imposts.[9]

While the resistence of Simancas was keeping the rebel army occupied in the north, the constable Miguel Lucas de Iranzo successfully resisted the seige of Jaén mounted by Pedro Girón. Girón and Pacheco, in addition to their persistent personal hostility to Lucas, had long wanted Jaén to round out Girón's Andalusian base. Girón in the early months of the war placed his forces before Jaén. The long and heroic defense kept Girón and his forces tied down in the south for longer than anticipated and allowed the royal army time to form up.[10]

The civil war was not a class struggle; both sides had supporters from all classes, though a majority of the towns favored Enrique. The divisions were not along geographic lines, nor were they based on ideological persuasions. Rather, the kingdom's mosaic of towns and cities, provinces, noble enclaves, and lands of the military orders shattered into its components. Scores of endemic frustrations and hostilities came to the surface and

8. Enríquez, *Crónica*, p. 147. This recalls an earlier refrain current at the time of Alvaro de Luna's loss of favor: "Esta es Burgos, cara de mona / Esta es Burgos, que no Escalona," Antonio Bermejo de la Rica, *El triste destino de Enrique IV y La Beltraneja* (Madrid, n.d. [1945]), p. 92.

9. Angel de la Plaza Bores, *Archivo General de Simancas: Guía del investigador* (Valladolid, 1962), p. xiv; RAH, *Salazar, leg.* M-76, fols. 86–97.

10. Palencia, *Crónica*, 1:183–84; *Hechos del Condestable Don Miguel Lucas de Iranzo*, ed. Juan de Mata Carriazo, Colección de crónicas españoles, no. 3 (Madrid, 1941), pp. 269–85; Miguel Angel Ladero Quesada, *Andalucía en el siglo XV: Estudios de historia política* (Madrid, 1973), p. 118.

anarchy reigned. As the war progressed and as both sides sought adherents and support, they adopted practical measures to reinforce their theoretical claims for allegiance. Enrique's group always cited morality and theology when calling on men to resist the rebels, while Alfonso's chieftains countered with the theory of justified revolt against an unjust king. But rarified arguments could not induce men to fight; support had to be bought and paid for. Enrique realized this and liberally rewarded his followers, granting the nobles lands and titles and making *hidalgos* of exceptional commoners.[11] The dissident faction had condemned this, saying that it weakened the kingdom, but what they were really resisting, and they knew it, was the dilution of the circle of privilege. Such were the realities of Castilian politics that the rebels in the name of Alfonso adopted the same tactics; the numbers of his grants can be seen in the table on p. 130. In April 1465 Alfonso gave Alvaro de Stúñiga the city of Trujillo and the title of duke.[12] As another example, in September 1465 we find the count of Benavente receiving from Alfonso the town of Portillo.[13] In June Alfonso had given Pedro Fajardo, the *adelantado mayor* of Murcia, the town and countryside of Cartagena.[14] Continually, requests were made for Enrique to arrest the growth of *hidalguía,* but at one stroke, Alfonso granted *hidalgo* status to fifteen men in the small town of Llanes.[15] Alfonso granted tax exemptions.[16] The rebels used exactly the same techniques they denounced the king for using.

For a determination of the royal actions in the civil war, the chroniclers are not too helpful. Their concern was the conflict of personalities, and they cared little about recording the changes in governmental policy. We are better served by the records of the requests made by the procurators of the sessions of the Cortes held at Ocaña in 1469 and Santa María de la Nieva in 1473, when the crown was petitioned to end or reverse the actions

11. In the first two years of the revolt, Enrique's most prominent supporters received the following titles: Alvar Pérez Osorio (marquis of Astorga), Garcí Alvarez de Toledo (duke of Alba de Tormes), Iñigo López de Mendoza (count of Tendilla), Diego Hurtado de Mendoza (count of Priego), Lorenzo Suárez de Mendoza (count of La Coruña del Conde), Alonso de Sotomayor (count of Belalcázar). Lowell W. Newton, "The Development of the Castilian Peerage" (unpublished Ph. D. dissertation, Tulane University, 1972), pp. 240–41.
12. *Colección diplomática*, doc. 111; AHN, *Osuna*, *leg.* 314, fol. 21.
13. AHN, *Osuna*, Condado de Benavente, *cajón* 1, nos. 1–2.
14. AGS, *Patronato Real, leg.* 58, fol. 29.
15. AGS, *Mercedes y privilegios*, *leg.* 3, fol. 108.
16. Salvador de Moxó, *La alcabala: Sobre sus orígenes, concepto y naturaleza* (Madrid, 1963), pp. 47–48.

undertaken in the period of unrest. The records of the Cortes are not verbatim transcripts of the proceedings, but rather they take the form of a summary, prepared after the fact, of the petitions of the assembly and the king's reactions. In both Cortes, the representatives showed concern over the unprecedented actions of the crown that had taken place during the disturbances. With careful scrutiny we are able to see a fairly clear outline of Enrique's policies as he faced the revolt, and we can thus supplement the rather meager image of these years offered by the chroniclers.

As the civil war broke out, Enrique moved to consolidate his support, and often he was forced to appeal to base instincts to garner it. He gained adherents by granting lands from the royal patrimony, by providing exemptions from taxation to individuals and towns, and by giving outright gifts of money.[17] He gave out patents of *hidalgo* status,[18] a practice the chroniclers mentioned and which is attested to by archival sources. To gain income he imposed new taxes while raising and extending existing ones. The taxes on sheep herds—the *servicio y montazgo*—were collected more often than usual; the 1473 Cortes mentioned two or three times per year as opposed to the normal annual payment. They were sometimes collected at unfamiliar places—quite understandably, since the usual collection point, Medina del Campo, was often outside royal jurisdiction.[19] To cover deficits in the treasury, royal notes (*cartas de espera*) were issued for future collection.[20] New officials were appointed as the previous officeholders deserted their posts.[21] Certain royal supporters—the Cortes mentioned *caballeros*, *escuderos*, and *donceles*—did not receive their full salaries.[22] Castles on the frontier of Granada were stripped of their garrisons and supplies to bolster royal forces, which Enrique explicitly stated to have been his motivation.[23] Through these actions the king indicated that he understood the dire necessities imposed on him by the rebellion and took the requisite steps to deal with them.

The grants and appointments the two factions made are too numerous to deal with individually. The table on p. 130 displays them graphically.

17. *Cortes*, vol. 3, Ocaña 1469: articles nos. 4–5, 6, pp. 773–81; Santa María de Nieva 1473: articles nos. 3–4, pp. 838–43, article no. 17, pp. 867–68.
18. Ibid., Santa María de Nieva 1473: article no. 14, pp. 863–66.
19. Ibid., Ocaña 1469: article no. 14, pp. 795–97; Santa María de Nieva 1473: article no. 18, pp. 868–69.
20. Ibid., Santa María de Nieva 1473: article no. 30, p. 880.
21. Ibid., Ocaña 1469: article no. 2, pp. 770–71, and no. 7, pp. 785–86; Santa María de Nieva 1473: article no. 6, pp. 845–49.
22. Ibid., Ocaña 1469: article no. 20, pp. 802–803.
23. Ibid., Ocaña 1469: article no. 22, p. 804.

Among the grants to individuals—lands and incomes mainly—Enrique gave twenty-nine in 1465, while Alfonso awarded thirty-nine in the same year. The number of Enrique's grants had increased in the year before the war as the situation worsened. Thereafter they leapt during the civil war and its aftermath. We can see the same policy in Enrique's grants to towns, religious establishments, and provinces. In addition to unspecified provisions and confirmations of existing privileges, he granted free fairs to Pontevedra, Cáceres, Roa, San Martín de Valdeiglesias, and Tordesillas.[24] Some grants to corporate bodies were honorific instead of economic. Guipúzcoa could call itself "the noble and loyal province." Cuenca, Jerez de la Frontera, Andújar, and Jaén could call themselves "very noble and very loyal," and Madrid, "noble and loyal," because of their early support for Enrique.[25] In both royal appointments of officials and grants of titles, the figures show similar advances. In 1465 Enrique appointed the greatest number of royal officials in his reign, as he was forced to replace officials who had joined the rebels.

Perhaps these grants would not have caused much impact on the royal government if Enrique had not granted so many concessions of royal taxes and income. Iñigo López de Mendoza, first count of Tendilla, in 1467 received a gift of all the mineral rights on his lands (a traditional regalian right) and the *tercias* of five town.[26] There were numerous grants of incomes; in 1465 alone Diego Arias de Avila, the chief royal accountant, received 41,000 maravedís in annuities (*juros*).[27] The total impact of Enrique's lavish grants was a significant decline in royal income. In his study of royal finance for the fifteenth century, Ladero Quesada calculated royal income for the period and used 1429 as a base year (index 100). In 1458 the index of Castilian income stood at 95, by 1465 it had fallen to 55, it stood at 60 when Enrique died, and it did not reach 95 again until 1491.[28] This is a sound and objective indication of the impact of the civil war and Enrique's attempt to deal with it. Perhaps the losses could have

24. RAH, *Salazar, leg.* O-16, fol. 222v; AHN, *Osuna, leg.* 1752, fol. 24; and documents cited in Juan Torres Fontes, *Itinerario de Enrique IV de Castilla* (Murcia, 1955), pp. 183, 187, 193-94, 202, 204-205.
25. Ladero Quesada, *Andalucía en el siglo XV*, p. 74; Torres Fontes, *Itinerario*, pp. 180, 190; Agustín Millares Carlo, ed., *Contribuciones documentales a la historia de Madrid* (Madrid, 1971), pp. 105-106.
26. RAH, *Salazar, leg.* M-1, fol. 19v; AHN, *Osuna, leg.* 1810, no. 16 (1-5). *Tercias* are defined in Chapter III, note 23.
27. AGS, *Mercedes y privilegios, leg.* 1, fols. 349, 682.
28. Miguel Angel Ladero Quesada, *La hacienda real de Castilla en el siglo XV* (La Laguna, 1973), pp. 43-44.

been recovered by rigorous actions to regain the grants, but even though Enrique agreed in two Cortes to revoke many of his concessions, he did not do so. Nor did his successors.[29]

Early in 1466 events became more favorable for the forces of Enrique. Twice the king offered a general pardon for a return to allegiance. In March Valladolid rose against the rebels and returned its obedience to the king. More important was the growing realization that Pope Paul II was disposed to favor the legal monarch. The propaganda war intensified as both sides presented opinions to the pope. For Enrique, the idea of justified rebellion was countered by the dean of Toledo, Francisco, who put forth the view that the only possible justification for depriving an anointed king of the throne was his conviction of the crime of heresy by a competent judge. The bishop of Ampurias and Juan López, master of theology, were called forth by Carrillo and worked up an appeal on the grounds that winners rule and the conquered are driven out. Paul II did not comment on the briefs, but sent Leonardo of Bologna to try to get both sides to resolve their quarrel.[30] Paul wrote Enrique to take heart and recall the betrayal and sufferings of Jesus. To the rebels the pope was blunter: they should desist and return to obedience to the legal king; anathema lay across the contrary path.[31]

Pacheco and Carrillo in the rebel band had very different ideas about the role Isabel was to play. Carrillo consistently worked for an Aragonese marriage for her, while Pacheco was exclusively concerned with her possible use as a tool to ensure rebel supremacy. She and her disposal by marriage were prime topics at the conference between the warring sides arranged by Archbishop Fonseca at his town of Coca for April 1466. The conference was a failure in its primary aim, which had been to arrange for the division of Castile into two zones, rebel and loyalist. The Mendozas were not a party to the conference and accordingly scorned it. But those present agreed that Isabel should be the bride of Pedro Girón, thus nullifying her usefulness in foreign affairs. Girón promised to use his influence to bring the rebels back to loyalty if Enrique would agree to the marriage. He did.[32]

29. On the limited nature of the attempt by Fernando and Isabel to deal with the situation, see Stephen Haliczer, "The Castilian Aristocracy and the Mercedes Reform of 1478-1482," *Hispanic American Historical Review* 55 (1975):449–67.

30. Galíndez, *Crónica*, pp. 277–80; Enríquez, *Crónica*, pp. 166–67.

31. Enríquez, *Crónica*, pp. 171–72.

32. Luis Suárez Fernández, "Los Trastámaras de Castilla y Aragón en el siglo XV (1407-74)," in vol. 15 of *Historia de España*, ed Ramón Menéndez Pidal (Madrid,

The young *infanta* was appalled by the thought of marriage with the uncouth Girón. She prayed for a day and a night, calling on God to prevent the marriage by killing either her or Girón. One wonders what emotion—relief, vindication, surprise—was uppermost when the news reached her that Girón had been stricken and died at Villarubia while leading a small army to take charge of her.[33] The credulous could point to heavenly intervention in the fortunate demise of Girón, as admirers of Isabel have consistently done.

The death of Girón took some of the impetus from the rebel program. There were many now on both sides who wanted a negotiated settlement. Fonseca devoted his entire efforts for nearly a year to achieve peace, but ultimately met failure. In May 1467, Juan II of Aragon, seeing the noble league as a possible instrument of Aragonese diplomacy, ostensibly put his support behind the rebels and sent as his agent Pierres de Peralta, a Navarrese of the Agramont faction who proved himself a worthy envoy. But Peralta carried a secret injunction to arrange a marriage for Juan's son Fernando with either Isabel or Pacheco's daughter Beatriz. Juan of Aragon was not one to leave any bet uncovered, although he preferred Isabel. Beltrán de la Cueva, Santillana, and Velasco threw all their support behind the king in late summer, asking only that he refrain from negotiations for a period of three months. Both sides launched an offensive, but when the adversaries clashed at the second battle of Olmedo on 20 August 1467, at best a draw resulted. The new papal legate—Antonio Jacobo de Veneris, bishop of León—arrived from Rome charged with settling the conflict. His comission clearly indicated the pope's favor for Enrique, and he was secretly armed with a bull of excommunication to be used against the rebels if all else failed. He tried to secure from Enrique a promise of pardon for the rebels, but the king balked. The rebels treated Veneris brusquely; they told him he had no right to negotiate since the pope had no temporal powers in Castile. Angered initially because Enrique allowed Veneris to negotiate at all and then because of the failure of the negotiations, the Mendozas, with Pedro González de Mendoza and possibly Iñigo López de Mendoza excepted, left the royal court.[34]

1964), p. 274; J.F. O'Callaghan, "Don Pedro Girón: Master of the Order of Calatrava," *Hispania* 21 (1961):383-85; Tarsicio de Azcona, *Isabel de Castilla: Estudio crítico sobre su vida y su reinado* (Madrid, 1964), pp. 109-110. The offers of pardons are cited in Torres Fontes, *Itinerario*, pp. 181, 193.

33. Palencia, *Crónica*, 1:203-204; O'Callaghan, "Don Pedro Girón," pp. 385-89.

34. Jaime Vicens Vives, *Historia crítica de la vida y reinado de Fernando II de Aragón* (Zaragoza, 1962), p. 232; Jaime Vicens Vives, *Juan II de Aragón (1398-1479):*

In mid-September 1467 Pedrarias Dávila turned Segovia over to the rebel forces and deprived the king of his most favored dwelling place. Realizing how psychologically dependent Enrique was upon Segovia, Pacheco decided to exploit the situation to his advantage. He approached the king and told him he could return the city to obedience, but at a high price; he demanded to be made master of Santiago. Enrique got his beloved Segovia back, but at the expense of greatly enlarging the power of the most dangerous man in the kingdom.[35]

Other cities were returning to obedience early in 1468, some of their own volition, others brought back by royal arms. In late spring Seville announced its allegiance to the crown, and Enrique received the homage of the knights of Valladolid. At the same time, through the means of a plot concocted by his supporters in the city, Enrique was able to regain Toledo.[36]

Meanwhile the bishopric of Sigüenza fell vacant and the king and the rebels fought over control of the new appointment. When the dean of Sigüenza, Diego López de Madrid, tried to assume the mitre, Pacheco and Carrillo, who rightly counted the dean as one of their partisans, tried to get the pope's approval. Pope Paul as always favored the legal king, and Enrique was able to secure the appointment for Pedro González de Mendoza.[37]

Monarquía y revolución en la España del siglo XV (Barcelona, 1953), p. 141; Enríquez, *Crónica*, pp. 166–67, 171–72; Luis Suárez Fernández, *Nobleza y monarquía: Puntos de vista sobre la historia castellana del siglo XV*, 2nd. ed. (Valladolid, 1975), pp. 217–18. On the battle of Olmedo, Diego de Valera, *Memorial de diversas hazañas*, ed. Juan de Mata Carriazo, Colección de crónicas españoles, no. 4 (Madrid, 1941), pp. 41–45. I have followed Vicens on Juan II's charge to Peralta, who Suárez believed was committed to the rebel band. Paul II's bull to Veneris is in AGS, *Patronato real, leg.* 11, fol 70. Also Justo Fernández Alonso, ed., *Legaciones y nunciaturas en España de 1466 a 1521*, 1: *1466-1486* (Rome, 1963), pp. 33–34. The agreement of Pedro González de Mendoza, Pedro de Velasco, and the marquis of Santillana was signed on 6 August 1467, AHN, *Osuna, leg.* 1860, fol. 17. Suárez stated that Pedro González de Mendoza was the only one of his family to side with the king, but about the same time (28 June 1467) Enrique signed a pact with Iñigo López de Mendoza: AHN, *Osuna, leg.* 1860, fol. 38.

35. Enríquez, *Crónica*, pp. 172–73.

36. Ibid., pp. 173–75; RAH, *Salazar, leg.* K-37, fols. 50–51; Eloy Benito Ruano, *Toledo en el siglo XV: Vida política* (Madrid, 1961), pp. 102–107. Suárez was incorrect in asserting that the cities returned to obedience without any action on the king's part. For Enrique's pardon of the citizens of Toledo, see *Colección diplomática*, doc. 146.

37. Galíndez, *Crónica*, p. 319.

A spirited fight in Alfonso's camp broke out in June over the marriage plans for the anti-king. Carrillo wanted to use the opportunity to secure Aragonese aid by having Alfonso marry Juana of Aragon. Pacheco objected; he feared Aragonese influence as much as he feared a strong Castilian monarchy. Pacheco also feared an Aragonese presence in Castile because many of the lands he and his late brother had secured were legally under the title of Juan II.[38] Early in July, the quarrel ended abruptly with the death of Alfonso in the small town of Cardeñosa near Avila, where he probably fell victim to an epidemic disease contracted while in Arévalo.[39]

The rebel band received the news of Alfonso's death with great concern. They were divided over what course to follow. Carrillo's faction wanted to proclaim Isabel as queen and continue the struggle, but a majority of the rebels were tired of the sacrifice of war. While the Salic prohibition on female succession had never been law in Castile, there was no favorable precedent, and the possibility of a young, untried woman succeeding to the throne gave pause to many. Eventually Pacheco's solution was acceptable to the majority. It called for renewed allegiance to Enrique as king, in exchange for his recognition of Isabel as his successor. Romantic tradition has Isabel herself adding momentum to the compromise by categorically stating that she regarded Enrique as the legal king and would not assume the crown while he lived, but Vicens Vives said that she had already been acting in a sovereign manner. She also took over certain towns, notably Medina del Campo, through the mediation of her follower Gonzalo Chacón. To keep Isabel from acting as a rival monarch, Enrique was ready to seize any chance of securing peace. To settle the problems besetting the kingdom, the leaders of the opposing factions agreed to meet in the countryside near Avila, in a plain known as Toros de Guisando because of the presence there of prehistoric statues of bulls.[40]

In mid-September 1468 the rival factions met at the appointed place. Isabel was accompanied by Pacheco and Carrillo and the bishops of Coria

38. Ibid., p. 324; Baltasar Cuartero y Huerta, *El pacto de los Toros de Guisando y la venta del mismo nombre* (Madrid, 1952), p. 31.

39. Enríquez, *Crónica,* p. 178. Palencia (*Crónica,* 1:249–50) said that Pacheco deliberately prolonged Alfonso's stay in Arévalo, hoping that he would catch the plague. When that failed, Pacheco had him poisoned. Juan Torres Fontes has shown that, according to Isabel herself, Alfonso died of "pestilencia," "La contratación de Guisando," *Anuario de Estudios Medievales* 2 (1965):404. See also Torres Fontes, *El príncipe Don Alfonso, 1465-1468* (Murcia, 1971), p. 89.

40. María Isabel del Val Valdivieso, *Isabel la Católica, Princesa (1468-1474)* (Valladolid, 1974), pp. 62–63; Vicens, *Fernando II,* pp. 234–42; Enríquez, *Crónica,* p. 178. Notification of Chacón's possession of Medina del Campo for Isabel is in AGS, *Diversos de Castilla, leg.* 40, fol. 49.

and Burgos. Enrique brought with him Diego and Alvaro de Stúñiga, Rodrigo Pimentel, Gabriel Manrique, Fonseca, and Diego López de Padilla. Both sides had armed troops on call. Enrique and Isabel greeted each other affectionately, but Carrillo fumed and said no respect should be shown the king until he had decided in favor of Isabel.[41] Enrique's adversaries were aided by the increasingly evil reputation of the queen. Whereas there was no evidence of the queen's adultery when the princess Juana was born, by this time she was separated from the king and pregnant.[42]

Aside from her renunciation of the throne, the agreement announced at Toros de Guisando was a victory for Isabel. She was named the hereditary princess and all previous provisions for the succession (i.e., Juana's rights) were to be declared void. Isabel agreed to be guided by Fonseca, Pacheco, and Alvaro de Stúñiga and no one else until she married. Enrique was to be regarded as king, lord, and foster father. No disservice to the king could be encouraged and Isabel was to work to bring the remaining rebels back into the fold. Enrique agreed to turn over to her the principality of Asturias and the cities and towns of Avila, Huete, Ubeda, Alcaraz, Molina, Medina del Campo, and Escalona. Any marriage plans had to originate with Enrique, but Isabel and her three guardians each had a veto over any such proposal. The pact stated that the king was *informed* that he had never been legally married to Juana the queen. Because of that and because for the last year the queen had been living promiscuously, the king should divorce or separate from her. Carrillo and Alvaro de Stúñiga were to hold Madrid in pawn for one year. If Enrique lived up to his part of the bargain, he would get it back; if not, Isabel was to get it.[43]

41. Enríquez, *Crónica*, pp. 178–79. Carrillo, at an unknown date, excommunicated Enrique IV and some of his lieutenants for having occupied two fortresses belonging to the archbishopric of Toledo: Fernández Alonso, ed., *Legaciones y nunciaturas*, 1:81–82. The excommunication was raised in 1472. The occasion of Carrillo's ire may have been as early as 28 June 1465, when Enrique revoked the grant he had made of a castle with 300 vassals near Cuenca: Torres Fontes, *Itinerario*, p. 179.
42. Suárez, *Nobleza y monarquía*, pp. 228–29; Val, *Isabel*, p. 72; Millares Carlo, ed., *Contribuciones documentales . . . Madrid*, pp. 201–203.
43. AGS, *Diversos de Castilla*, *leg.* 9, fol. 66; *Colección diplomática*, doc. 152; Cuartero, *Toros de Guisando*, pp. 40–44. Both Vicens (*Fernando II*, pp. 234–42) and Azcona (*Isabel*, pp. 122–29) stress the limited nature of the agreements. Val (*Isabel*, pp. 79–80) has found a contemporary copy of the agreement in the archive of the duke of Frías, thereby helping to allay the suspicions that the text of the Toros agreement may have been a later forgery.

It is interesting that nowhere was the question of Juana's paternity squarely faced. It was implied that she was not the king's daughter, but only the consistently unreliable Palencia states that at Toros de Guisando Juana was definitely branded as a bastard. Yet the Isabelline faction proposed the idea that Juana was illegitimate, not because she had been fathered by someone other than the king, but because Enrique and his queen had not been legally married. This argument commands more interest and attention, since it can be based at least partially upon documentary evidence. Because Enrique of Castile and Juana of Portugal were related, the question arose of whether a papal bull of dispensation was necessary for a valid marriage. Under Portuguese influence, Nicholas V had issued a commission to three bishops—Alfonso Carrillo, Alfonso de Fonseca, and Alfonso of Valladolid—to judge the case, and if they agreed it was necessary, to issue the required dispensation. The commission is extant, but evidence that the commissioners issued such a formal dispensation is not. Azcona in his careful study of the problem denied the imputation that the marriage was invalid. It must have been considered canonically correct, or the warm relations between the papal and Castilian courts would have been impossible. Fonseca and Carrillo (Alfonso of Valladolid had died) were present at the Toros meeting and did nothing to challenge the charge that the marriage was invalid. This, not the rumors that Enrique had not fathered Juana, was the real basis on which Isabel built her right to succeed Enrique, and if the king and his supporters formally countered it, the documents have not survived. The Toros agreement was also helpful to Isabel since it provided no sanctions against her in the event that she did not follow its provisions to the letter. Her marriage to Fernando, contracted in direct opposition to the clause requiring Enrique's approval, did not invalidate the terms.[44] The supporters of Isabel, of course, never recognized the unilateral action by the king when he overturned the Toros agreement in 1470, and after the king's death the superior political position of Fernando and Isabel rendered such considerations moot.

The *grandes* present accepted the agreement in the name of the three estates. On 23 September the king called upon other nobles to come and give obedience to Isabel as the legal heir. On the next day Enrique formally recognized his sister. Carrillo was still dissatisfied, and Isabel and the

44. Palencia, *Crónica*, 1:263; Azcona, *Isabel*, pp. 30–34. Leaning toward Isabel's side are Vicente Rodríquez Valencia and Luis Suárez Fernández, *Matrimonio y derecho sucesorio de Isabel la Católica* (Valladolid, 1960), especially p. 123.

papal legate had to write him formal letters urging him to return to obedience to Enrique. On Enrique's side, the Mendozas refused to follow the provisions against Queen Juana and wrote to the pope in the name of the queen expressing discontent, while opposing Isabel's recognition.[45]

Enrique's willingness to compromise needs examination. There is a complete absence of documentary evidence concerning his motivations, but considering the king's character and the situation he faced, several plausible conjectures arise. A strong factor was his eternal dislike of strife and discord, and this was coupled with his compelling desire to regain his beloved Segovia, which the rebels had again recaptured. He had not been compelled to deny his paternity in the case of Juana, only to set aside her right to the throne. This may seem a fine distinction, but it avoided any definite statements about his virility. Despite the political quarrel, Enrique and his sister Isabel had maintained a strong mutual affection. The clauses of Isabel's letters stressing her love were not mere formalities. One of the few personal letters we have from Enrique was addressed to Isabel. In gracious phrases he eloquently expressed his feelings:

> Certainly your ladyship can be sure that there is nothing I could do to serve and please you that I would not do for my sister. . . . I beseech you to always remember me, because you do not have any person in this world who loves you as much as I do.[46]

Such an attitude no doubt encouraged him to trust her pledge to regard him as rightful ruler and not challenge his sovereignty. Once the active revolt was dispelled, he could hope to rebuild his support and overturn the provisions of the pact, which in fact he did in October 1470. So it is very likely that Enrique saw the agreement of Toros de Guisando as a temporary, tactical retreat, by no means a final disposition of the political situation in Castile.

But if he made the best of a difficult situation by accepting the agreement, Enrique blundered in the worst possible way by allowing Pacheco to return to his circle of advisers. Nothing in the sources helps to explain this disastrous move. The king's supporters were mystified and angered.

45. Letter to the *grandes*, AGS, *Diversos de Castilla*, *leg*. 9, fol. 64; Enrique's recognition, AGS, *Patronato Real*, *leg*. 7, fol. 112; the concord between Isabel and Carrillo, *Colección diplomática*, doc. 153; Iñigo López de Mendoza's letter, *Colección diplomática*, doc. 156, and Antonio de la Torre and Luis Suárez Fernández, eds., *Documentos referentes a las relaciones con Portugal durante el reinado de los Reyes Católicos*, 1 (Valladolid, 1958), pp. 59–65.

46. Enrique IV, letter to Isabel, undated (but probably before July 1468), printed in Azcona, *Isabel*, p. 112.

Pacheco had been an acknowledged leader of the rebel faction, and as such was hated by Enrique's partisans; many of the rebel faction hated him too, for that matter. Why then did Enrique take him back? The question cannot be answered satisfactorily. They had been friends since adolescence, and we have seen that some even imply a homosexual relationship between them. Enrique may have felt that with the talent Pacheco had for gaining adherents to a troublesome rebel faction, he could prove equally successful in working for the royal camp. Perhaps, but in any case Pacheco was not willing to operate in that manner. It is an understatement to say that Enrique's faithful partisans were dismayed by the arrival of Pacheco, and from that moment dates the exodus of the former associates of the king. The more faithful said they would serve Enrique during his life, but after his death Isabel, not Juana, would have their support. Others immediately began working for Isabel. From this point onward, the balance slowly but resolutely swung to the side of the future Catholic queen. By the time of his death, Enrique was virtually denuded of powerful support, and it was mainly his own fault.

Pacheco's first plot after regaining royal favor was to press for the marriage of Isabel to the widowed Portuguese king Afonso V. The bargain included the princess Juana; she was to marry Afonso's son. Some of the *grandes* agreed to the idea, but the Mendozas, stung by Enrique's acceptance of the hated Pacheco, held back. The Mendozas believed Pacheco was only concerned with getting Juana under his control. They were undoubtedly right, for by this time it is highly likely that Pacheco realized Isabel was not at all inclined to be his willing tool.[47]

It is not clear just how early Isabel was resolved on the marriage with Fernando of Aragon (at this time bearing the title of King of Sicily), but the agreement must have been undertaken by the end of 1468. Vicens believed it was reached even before the death of Alfonso. Just at that time Pierres de Peralta (Juan II's Castilian operative) was rounding up support for Isabel. From Enrique's staunchest supporters—Velasco, Santillana, and Pedro González de Mendoza—Peralta got a secret agreement that they would recognize Isabel as the successor to Enrique. They would remain loyal during the king's lifetime, but would take no action to help place Juana on the throne.[48]

In the spring of 1469 Enrique, influenced by Pacheco, decided that the bonds between himself and his followers and the other *grandes* should

47. Enríquez, *Crónica*, pp. 180–81.

48. Suárez, *Nobleza y monarquía*, pp. 233–34; Vicens, *Juan II de Aragón*, p. 314.

be made stronger, so Enrique and a group of nobles signed a confederation. The signatories included friends and enemies: Fonseca, Pacheco, Alvaro de Stúñiga, Diego Hurtado de Mendoza, Beltrán de la Cueva, Pedro González de Mendoza, and Pedro de Velasco. Most received grants and privileges.[49] On Enrique's part this was probably a great mistake, since already in mid-March the procurators of the kingdom had formally petitioned the monarch not to alienate any more of the royal patrimony.[50] There was a Cortes held at Ocaña shortly afterward, but it was weak—only ten towns were represented and Carrillo and his followers declined to attend. Acting as spokesman for the king, Fonseca read a statement promising royal justice, economic and administrative order, and a stop to the granting of *hidalguía*. The procurators went home without judging for Isabel as heir.[51]

With the end of the civil war, Enrique's response to the rebels was overly charitable, as he worked vigorously to secure support. Many, including García Franco, Juan Ponce de León, and Gonzalo de Saavedra, received pardons.[52] Pedro de Stúñiga had been with Alfonso at Avila and in the course of the war had seized the castle of Burgos; Enrique forced him to give up the castle but compensated him for it.[53] Fadrique Manrique in 1469 got perpetual possession of the offices of *alcalde mayor* and *alcaide de los alcázares* of Ecija.[54] The count of Benavente, Juan Pimentel, in 1468 and 1469 got the towns of Portillo and Castromocho and the castle of Villalba.[55] Juan Ponce de León, count of Arcos de la Frontera, had his possessions confirmed in 1469,[56] and Enrique Enríquez, the admiral's brother, received a privilege.[57] Pacheco and his family especially gained. The marquis himself received annuities in 1468 and 1472 and the town and castle of Escalona in 1470.[58] Both his son and daughter received gifts.[59] Pacheco's nephew, Rodrigo Téllez Girón, who succeeded his father as master of Calatrava, received the royal offices of *notario mayor* and

49. Suárez, *Nobleza y monarquía*, p. 236; AHN, *Osuna*, *leg*. 1860, fol. 20.
50. *Codoin*, 87:482.
51. Galíndez, *Crónica*, p. 340; Suárez, *Nobleza y monarquía*, p. 232.
52. AHN, *Osuna*, *leg*. 118, fol. 7; *leg*. 417, fol. 12; *leg*. 1635, fol. 1.
53. Ibid., *leg*. 216, fol. 8.
54. RAH, *Salazar*, *leg*. M-117, *hojas* 90–105.
55. AHN, *Osuna*, *leg*. 417, fol. 11; *leg*. 518, fol. 4.
56. RAH, *Salazar*, *leg*. B-3, fol. 364v.
57. Ibid., *leg*. M-49, fols. 206–207v.
58. Ibid., *leg*. D-14, fol. 120; AHN, *Osuna*, *leg*. 1735, fol. 2b; Torres Fontes, *Itinerario*, p. 218. He also got, at an unknown date, the alum mines of Murcia, BN, Ms. 887, no. 20, fols. 423–425v.
59. RAH, *Salazar*, *leg*. M-90, *hojas* 64–65, 102–11v; Torres Fontes, *Itinerario*, p. 232.

camarero mayor de los paños and the town of Gumiel.[60]

Staunch supporters during the civil war were also favored. Beltrán de la Cueva, who became the duke of Alburquerque in the first year of the war, received the *montazgo* (royal transit tax) income from Arroyo de Castaño in 1469 and the town of Codosera in 1472.[61] The Mendoza family gained a great deal. The head of the family, Diego Hurtado de Mendoza, won possession of Guadalajara.[62] Pedro González de Mendoza got the town of Alfaro.[63] The count of Tendilla, Iñigo López de Mendoza, was granted La Guardia (in Navarre), Peñalcázar, and a number of vassals in Huete.[64] Their brother Lorenzo received three towns.[65]

One of the most serious charges to be made legitimately against Enrique IV concerns his policy on grants. Forced by circumstances to buy support, he made too many concessions, and he failed to check his generosity when the war was over. Nothing he did damaged the fiscal position of the crown more.

In early May 1469, conditions in Andalusia called the king southward. As was his right as guardian, he told Isabel to remain in Ocaña and hold in abeyance any decision on her marriage. She had already declined a Portuguese offer tendered by the archbishop of Lisbon on behalf of Afonso V and by now she was firmly resolved on the marriage with Fernando, a plan being ably negotiated by Peralta and Carrillo.[66] At about the same time, Avila gave its backing to Isabel.[67]

Enrique, accompanied by Pacheco, Fonseca, and Pedro González de Mendoza, entered the south and found that the political tide was running against him because of his association with Pacheco. In Jaén, Miguel Lucas de Iranzo, who had control of the city, refused to allow Pacheco to enter. Enrique was welcome, but his traitorous minister was not. He found a similar situation in Córdoba, then under the control of Alonso de Aguilar,

60. AHN, *Osuna*, *leg*. 3, fol. 2; *leg*. 79, fol. 9; *leg*. 105, fol. 11.

61. Torres Fontes, *Itinerario*, pp. 227, 250.

62. To complete the Mendoza control of the Infantado, Pacheco and his son had to be persuaded to relinquish their holdings in the area. AHN, *Osuna*, *leg*. 1724, fol. 13; *leg*. 1726, fol. 10; *leg*. 1727, fol. 9; *leg*. 1873, fol. 7; RAH, *Salazar*, *leg*. M-9, fol. 74–74v, 218–19, 304v–306; *leg*. M-13, fols. 91–93v; *leg*. M-20, fols. 51–51v; *leg*. M-25, fols. 89–89v; Torres Fontes, *Itinerario*, p. 225.

63. AHN, *Osuna*, *leg*. 2266, fol. 4.

64. RAH, *Salazar*, *leg*. M-1, fols. 21v–22; *leg*. M-9, fols. 347–55v.

65. Torres Fontes, *Itinerario*, p. 221.

66. Enríquez, *Crónica*, p. 185.

67. AGS, *Diversos de Castilla*, *leg*. 9, fol. 63.

who also was very discontented with Pacheco.[68] In the same city Enrique gave a blanket pardon to the Ponce de León family.[69]

While in Córdoba, Enrique was visited by an ambassador from Louis XI. According to Galíndez, the French king was anxious to re-establish friendly relations with Castile. France's economy had been hurt because Enrique had barred Castilian merchants from France after the Catalan imbroglio and had signed an agreement with England. To re-establish Franco-Castilian concord, the French envoy was empowered to negotiate a marraige between Isabel and Charles, duke of Berry and Guienne. Enrique by now had got word that Isabel, urged on by Carrillo and Fadrique Enríquez (Fernando's maternal grandfather), had left Ocaña to be in Madrigal, where she was less under royal control. The French cardinal followed her there and pressed for her agreement. She declined in such a manner that the ambassador became angry and turned his favor to Juana as a more suitable marriage partner for Charles.[70]

Isabel then precipitated matters by deciding that the marriage with Fernando must be concluded swiftly. She left Madrigal and established herself in Valladolid to await the arrival of Fernando. The famous ceremony took place on 18 October 1469, arranged by Carrillo and Peralta with the aid of a hastily forged document alleged to be a papal dispensation to allow the closely related couple to marry within the proscribed degrees of kinship.[71] Over two weeks before in Zaragoza Fernando had pledged not to make any grants in the Castilian kingdom without Isabel's consent; it is clear from the start that Isabel took pains to guarantee her position.[72] With the deed accomplished and having achieved a secure position, Isabel endeavored to define her stance regarding Enrique. Her policy, and we must regard it as more likely her own than that of her disparate advisers and friends, was to work at all cost toward a legal transmission of the crown. It was necessary for her to make herself independent of Enrique, but not to arouse his anger to a dangerous point. With this in mind, she

68. Galíndez, *Crónica*, pp. 345–46.
69. AHN, *Osuna*, *leg.* 118, fol. 7.
70. Enríquez, *Crónica*, pp. 184–85; Valera, *Diversas hazañas*, pp. 154–55. Suárez erred in believing that Isabel fooled her visitor and that he left without hostility toward the princess. *Nobleza y monarquía*, p. 234.
71. Palencia, *Crónica*, 1:296–97; Vicens, *Fernando II*, pp. 256–63; Vicens, *Juan II de Aragón*, p. 319. The forged bull is in AGS, *Patronato Real*, *leg.* 49, fol. 40. The agreement between Carrillo and Peralta is in *Colección diplomática*, doc. 160. See also Val, *Isabel*, pp. 191–97.
72. AGS, *Patronato Real*, *leg.* 7, fol. 106.

wrote her brother telling him of the marriage; she would remain loyal, she said, but she must have the town of Arévalo returned to her. She inserted a pointed reminder of the agreement of Toros de Guisando. This and her other letters to Enrique were masterful. They touched on affection and loyalty, but firmly reminded the king that she was a force to be dealt with very carefully.[73] He needed no reminding. He knew her potential as a focus of discontent; he had occupied a similar position as prince of Asturias, and only Alfonso's death had ended his threat.

The news of the marriage reached Enrique in the south, where he was busy with international as well as domestic problems. In a move quite in keeping with his intelligent Granadan policy, he met with the Muslim ruler of Málaga. The two entered into a pact to work against the king of Granada. In Carmona, however, the king's luck did not hold, and Pacheco's presence brought him down once again. Pacheco held two of Carmona's three fortresses and wanted the third, then held by Gómez Méndez de Sotomayor. Enrique tried to help Pacheco dispossess Gómez. This was disastrous, because Gómez was the kinsman of many nobles of Seville, among them the duke of Medina Sidonia. Open insurrection broke out in Seville, led by the nobles and joined by the populace. When Enrique arrived to survey the scene, Medina Sidonia bluntly told him that neither he nor his followers would work with Pacheco. The strong implication was that they would not work with Enrique either, as long as he persisted in retaining Pacheco.[74] In the matter of Juana, at least, the lines of interest of Pacheco and the king converged. Pacheco wanted Juana to serve as the figurehead of his movement. Enrique now wanted desparately to secure the throne for his daughter, and he was willing to accommodate himself to Pacheco's goal to ensure his own. Prospects for Enrique were not bleak. It is well known that the newly married Fernando and Isabel were desperately short of money. In fact, Juan of Aragon supported them until Isabel became queen.[75] Enrique still enjoyed a large residue of loyalty in the kingdom, and all the towns of Castile were loyal except for Valladolid, Tordesillas, Olmedo, and Sepúlveda. The international reputation of the king was still high. Galíndez reported that Jean of Anjou was willing to work with the Catalans against Juan II because the Aragonese king was old and poor and possessed the enmity of Enrique of Castile. With these

73. Enríquez, *Crónica*, pp. 187–90; RAH, *Salazar, leg.* F-20, fols. 139v–147v.

74. Enríquez, *Crónica*, pp. 195–96.

75. ACA, *Cancillería, Diversorum sigilii secreti*, R3393, nos. 12, 35–36. Val, *Isabel*, pp. 189, 275–77, 309–310.

points in mind, Pacheco and the king put all their hopes on securing a suitable marriage for Juana. Their first hope was the familiar figure of Charles, duke of Berry and Guienne.[76]

While the French negotiations were being conducted, two promising events occurred. Royal forces regained Valladolid, and the membership of the order of Alcántara revolted in favor of the king. Gómez de Cáceres, master of the order, had risen against the king, but the majority of the members fell in with the *clavero* Alonso de Monrroy and deposed their leader.[77]

Therefore, by October 1470, the king felt strong enough to overthrow the agreement of Toros de Guisando. At a meeting on the Campo de Santiago, the agreement was annulled and Juana again named heir to the throne. She entered into an agreement of marriage with Charles of Berry. The Franch ambassador, no doubt conversant with the rumor-mongers of Castile, insisted on a sworn statement by both king and queen that the child was really fathered by Enrique. Bad luck killed the brief hope for Juana's future contained in these negotiations when Charles of Berry died shortly afterward. The luster of the proposed marriage had already suffered when Louis XI, Charles's brother, was presented with a son.[78]

In the same month, Fernando and Isabel produced a child, proving that their marriage was a fruitful one and that with Isabel as queen, questions of paternity should not arise. In Fernando, Isabel had a strong male partner, a king in his own right, and this fact removed the stigma of female succession from her and placed it on the still unmarried Juana. Isabel's task now was to sit back, making few overt moves, and quietly bring the *grandes* over to her side while working for the legal transmission of the crown. She sent a circular letter to the Castilian cities indicating her position,[79] and by making grants to followers, she was acting as if she were already in power.[80] The future *Reyes Católicos* turned out to be masterful

76. Galíndez, *Crónica*, pp. 371–72; 374–75.
77. Alonso Maldonaldo, *Hechos del Maestre de Alcántara, Don Alonso de Monrroy*, ed. Antonio R. Rodríquez Moñino (Madrid, 1935), pp. 42, 66–71, 95, 134.
78. Vicens, *Fernando II*, pp. 279–82. The document changing the succession from Isabel to Juana is in AGS, *Diversos de Castilla*, *leg*. 9, fol. 65; a similar document appears in RAH, *Salazar*, *leg*. M-13, fols. 102–104.
79. RAH, *Colección Velázquez*, leg. 4, fol. 168; *Colección diplomática*, doc. 178.
80. In 1470 Isabel was confirming *mercedes*, AGS, *Registro general del sello*, *leg*. 1, fols. 11–12. In 1468 she granted the alum mines of Alcaraz to Diego López de Haro and in 1469 signed a compact with Fernando de Rojas y Sandoval, 2nd. count of Castro: RAH, *Salazar*, *leg*. M-45, fols. 223v–24v, 303–303v.

politicians. In the last years of Enrique's reign, the king saw his followers desert one by one to his adversaries, as he helplessly stood by and watched.

In August 1471, Sixtus IV became pope and changed the Castilian policy of Rome by transferring his favor to Fernando and Isabel and sending as his legate Rodrigo Borja, the Valencian who would become Pope Alexander VI. The most tangible evidence of papal support for the prince and the princess was an *ex post facto* dispensation for their marriage, which Sixtus issued on 1 December 1471.[81]

Enrique now was desperate to provide a husband for his discredited daughter. He had the Portuguese sounded out on a marriage between the aging Afonso V and Juana. Enrique and Afonso met for the last time between Badajoz and Yelpes in March 1472. The Portuguese monarch refused to agree to the proposal and was quite frank in expressing his reason; he distrusted Pacheco.[82]

With hope of finding a spouse for his daughter waning, the king seized on an idea of Pacheco to arrange a marriage for Juana with Enrique Fortuna, a grandson of Fernando de Antequera and son of Enrique, one of the old Infantes of Aragon. Years before, Pierres de Peralta had tried to win Pacheco over to the Aragonese side by proposing to marry Enrique Fortuna to Pacheco's daughter Beatriz. Pacheco had not agreed to the plan. This time Fortuna's name was pressed by the count of Benavente and Pacheco. Enrique was willing, and Fortuna came to Castile. That proved a blunder, for his vacuity and, more important, his lack of money or connections were readily apparent to the Castilians. The negotiations were allowed to die.[83] Juana's future was still unsettled, and Enrique's own power continued to ebb steadily away.

Pedro González de Mendoza was the most prominent member of his powerful family. Enrique had steadily advanced him, getting his first

81. AGS, *Patronato Real*, *leg.* 12, fol. 32; Suárez, *Nobleza y monarquía*, pp. 240–41.

82. Enríquez, *Crónica*, pp. 211–12; Galíndez, *Crónica*, pp. 408–14. The chronology of Galíndez broke down toward the end of the chronicle; he put the date of the meeting in 1471. Torres Fontes gave the date of 4 March: *Itinerario*, p. 251. Suárez, *Nobleza y monarquía*, p. 241, said that it was in May. In an undated letter to Afonso V of Portugal, the duke of Berganza gave his king a bleak report on the situation in Castile and mentioned the possibility of Enrique's impotence. If this letter was received before the meeting, it could well have influenced the Portuguese king: BN, Ms. 2420, no. 1, fols. 1-6v.

83. Galíndez, *Crónica*, pp. 431–34; Valera, *Diversas hazañas*, pp. 76, 79; Suárez, "Los Trastámaras," pp. 290, 307-308; *Coleccion diplomática*, docs. 194-95; Val, *Isabel*, pp. 303-307.

diocese for him and giving him more important posts as they fell vacant. Pedro González had been loyal, but his ambition decreed his continued dissatisfaction. He conceived the idea of getting a cardinal's biretta for himself and pressed Enrique to help him just at the time when the new pope Sixtus was turning away from the Castilian king. Fernando of Aragon was in a position to do something for the aspiring bishop and persuaded Mendoza that only through his influence with the legate Borja could Mendoza gain the cardinalate. Enrique was actually working toward the same goal for the bishop, but by March 1472 when Mendoza achieved his appointment, he was convinced it was all due to Fernando. The new cardinal used his influence willingly to wean his relatives away from Enrique. His task was made easy because Fernando was a relative of the Mendozas. In the last years of Enrique's reign, the Mendoza family agreed that while they would not oppose the king, they would do nothing to help his daughter after his death.[84]

The pattern was similar for the rest of the high nobility. We can see at least three motives at work as Enrique's supporters inexorably deserted: opposition to Pacheco, a belief that Fernando and Isabel would prove better governors, and a desire for personal gain. Of the three, distrust and dislike of Pacheco was undoubtedly the most important.

In February 1473 a confederation was signed between the duke of Medina Sidonia and the future monarchs. Around the same time Andrés de Cabrera went over to Isabel. He was angry over Pacheco's insistence on obtaining the fortresses of Madrid and Segovia, which the *mayordomo mayor* Cabrera held.[85] Death further reduced the ranks of the supporters of Enrique; Miguel Lucas de Iranzo died, as did Fonseca of Seville. The marquis of Santillana changed his allegiance because of Fernando's support in the struggle between the marquis and the count of Benavente over the possession of Carrión.[86]

In 1473 Enrique undertook his last administrative reform of any consequence. This was the reorganization of the *Hermandades*. Meeting at Villacastín in July, the king and the leaders of the local brotherhoods formed the disorganized units of the *Hermandades* into a truly national

84. Suárez, *Nobleza y monarquía*, p. 240; Fernández Alonso, ed., *Legaciones y nunciaturas*, 1:85–86.
85. Galíndez, *Crónica*, p. 428.
86. Ibid., pp. 427–28, 432–33, 445–47.

police force. Enrique's successors would make great use of this restructured body.[87]

At the end of December 1473 and the beginning of January 1474, Enrique and his sister undertook a series of meetings in Segovia. Through the mediation of Andrés de Cabrera and his wife Beatriz de Bobadilla, and the count of Benavente, Enrique agreed to meet his sister in the *alcázar* (fortress) of Segovia.[88] The meeting between Enrique and Isabel was cordial, even loving, as Enríquez reported. Isabel expressed her firm desire to succeed her brother, but she could get no confirmation of this from him. Still, the meeting went so well that the king decided to have Isabel and her husband to dinner some days later. At the meal, Fernando sat next to Isabel, who was placed beside the king at the head of the table. After dinner the party retired to another room to hear music. In the middle of the recital Enrique was stricken with a severe pain in his side and was forced to go to bed. For several days he was very ill and although he partially recovered, for the rest of his life he was subject to diarrhea, vomiting, and the passage of blood in the urine. Fernando and Isabel remained in the city during the worst of the illness, visiting the king and pleading with him to recognize Isabel as his successor. Pacheco got word of the king's illness, and, fearing the machinations of the Isabelline faction, he secretly moved up troops, planning to take the strong points of the city and imprison Cabrera, Fernando, and Isabel. Cabrera discovered the plan, however, and closed the city to Pacheco.[89]

All this raises the fascinating question of whether Fernando and Isabel decided to secure their position by poisoning the king. It must have been apparent from Enrique's attitude that he was not in the least inclined to recognize his sister; even in his extreme pain he steadfastly refused. Through Cabrera, Fernando and Isabel would control the city, and Segovia also housed Enrique's major treasury. Most historians pass over the dinner episode lightly. Of those who mention it, Orestes Ferrara dismissed the imputation of poisoning on the weak grounds that poisoning was unknown

87. Suárez, "Los Trastámaras," p. 310; Marvin Lunenfeld, *The Council of the Santa Hermandad: A Study of the Pacification Forces of Ferdinand and Isabella* (Coral Gables, Florida, 1970), p. 22; Torres Fontes, *Itinerario*, p. 260.

88. *Crónica incompleta de los Reyes Católicos (1469-1476)*, ed. Julio Puyol (Madrid, 1934), pp. 112–22, reports the lengthy conversation between Beatriz de Bobadilla and the king. Cabrera was willing to consider supporting Fernando and Isabel because he had suffered from Pacheco's machinations. Val, *Isabel*, pp. 262–64, 306.

89. Enríquez, *Crónica*, pp. 217–18; Galíndez, *Crónica*, pp. 444–45.

in Castile, but perhaps he was leaving the question open to another interpretation by implying that it was not unknown in other countries.[90] Gregorio Marañón, historian and physician, also declined to make a definitive statement, but noted that the symptoms of Enrique's ailment most closely resemble arsenic poisoning.[91] If Fernando and Isabel did plot the king's death, they were foiled in their attempt at a rapid coup. Enrique recovered, but the aftereffects of the episode at Segovia undoubtedly hastened his death before the year was out.

The end was obviously approaching, and Enrique did everything he could to ensure an orderly succession for his daughter. Unfortunately, his actions only further alienated those nobles who could have been Juana's supporters. There was a major defection from the opposing camp in the person of Carrillo, who quit Isabel's group when he discovered that he could no longer dictate to his erstwhile protegés. Enrique called upon Pedro González de Mendoza to help in the succession crisis, but the cardinal, firmly committed to the opposition, pleaded with the king to consider the inevitable bloodshed that would result from a disputed succession and not to insist on Juana as his heir.[92]

Juan Pacheco died on 4 October 1474 and on his deathbed entrusted the cause of Juana to his son, Diego López Pacheco, second marquis of Villena. The great plum of the mastership of Santiago was now vacant, and the more important nobles were scrambling wildly for it. Practically everyone of substance wanted it: the duke of Medina Sidonia, the count of Benavente, the marquis of Santillana, the count of Paredes, Beltrán de la Cueva, and (proving himself his father's son) Diego López Pacheco. Enrique favored the latter, most likely in view of the marquis's partisanship of Juana, and Carrillo helped the king to get it granted. For the unsuccessful contenders, understandably, this was the last straw. Virtually all the great nobles thereafter were allied with or sympathetic to Isabel and her husband.[93]

In early winter, with his afflictions bothering him, Enrique went to Madrid for some hunting in the forest of El Pardo. One afternoon he fell

90. Orestes Ferrara, *Un pleito sucesorio: Enrique IV, Isabel de Castilla y La Beltraneja* (Madrid, 1945), p. 334.

91. Gregorio Marañón, *Ensayo biológico sobre Enrique IV de Castilla y su tiempo*, 10th ed. (Madrid, 1964), pp. 73–74. Pacheco tried to persuade Enrique that he had been poisoned. Val, *Isabel*, p. 324.

92. Galíndez, *Crónica*, pp. 452, 456.

93. Ibid., pp. 454–55; Enríquez, *Crónica*, pp. 220–21; Val, *Isabel*, pp. 346–50.

VIII

LEGACIES

With the king dead the struggle for power broke out in earnest. In Segovia on 13 December 1474, without waiting for Fernando to return from Aragon, Isabel took the crown in a ceremony hastily prepared by Andrés de Cabrera. The long efforts of Fernando and Isabel to secure bonds of allegiance in the kingdom were finally successful, and at the beginning of the war of succession they had the support of most of the great families, together with a majority of the Castilian towns. In a series of formal agreements signed in December of 1474 and January of 1475, the nobles pledged their backing. Even Beltrán de la Cueva came over in January, after he obtained a guarantee of his titles and possessions. The arrangements were on a quid pro quo basis: in return for their political and military support, the nobles received ratification of their holdings and titles.[1]

The king's daughter had small support in Castile. The list of her followers was short and unimpressive: Diego López Pacheco (second marquis of Villena), Juan de Stúñiga (nominally the master of Alcántara), Rodrigo Téllez Girón (nominally the master of Calatrava), Pedro Portocarrero, Diego López de Stúñiga, and a few others.[2] Alfonso Carrillo, the crusty archbishop of Toledo, wavered between both factions. While there were pockets of resistence elsewhere in the kingdom, the holdings of Juana's faction were mainly concentrated in the southern Meseta and in the west of the kingdom along the Portuguese frontier. This made Portuguese assis-

1. Luis Suárez Fernández, "La guerra de sucesión," in vol. 17, part 1, of *Historia de España*, ed. Ramón Menéndez Pidal (Madrid, 1969), pp. 89–91. The agreement of 27 December 1474 between Fernando and Isabel and Pedro González de Mendoza, plus the constable, the admiral, and the count of Benavente is printed in *Colección diplomática*, doc. 207. The sequestration of rebel goods is in ibid., doc. 209.

   The best biography of Isabel is Tarsicio de Azcona, *Isabel de Castilla: Estudio crítico sobre su vida y su reinado* (Madrid, 1964); of Fernando, Jaime Vicens Vives, *Historia crítica de la vida y reinado de Fernando II de Aragón* (Zaragoza, 1962). Felipe Fernández-Armesto has provided a sound popular account in English: *Ferdinand and Isabella* (New York, 1975).

2. *Crónica incompleta de los Reyes Católicos (1469-1476)*, ed. Julio Puyol (Madrid, 1934), pp. 135–36.

tance easier to secure, but the limited territorial base allowed their adversaries to concentrate their forces.

Everything indicates the pragmatic, non-ideological nature of the aristocratic proclivities; the *grandes* followed the standard of whoever could secure the best position for them. For some high nobles, Fernando and Isabel had come to represent their best hope, while others saw their victory as inevitable and wished to join the winning side. Orestes Ferrara branded Isabel's succession as a usurpation based on superior military force.[3] It can well be considered a usurpation, but we can better say that her faction enjoyed superior military force because for years before the death of Enrique IV they had doggedly pursued an intelligent political program and that their victory was almost assured because of it.

By the end of 1476 most of the nobles had reconciled themselves with Fernando and Isabel. Among the last to hold out were Diego López Pacheco and Archbishop Carrillo. Carrillo gave his allegiance in September; thereafter he never regained his former prominence. López Pacheco signed an agreement at the same time, but it was broken several times in the next years. The final settlement with López Pacheco, reached only in 1480, was not too different from that of other nobles. In return for his allegiance to Fernando and Isabel, he was able to keep many of his estates, although they were carved into a number of separate blocs, and he lost some of the principal towns his father had held.[4] During the period immediately after Enrique's death numerous towns in Castile had joined the couple's camp, because they feared alienation from the crown to noble control.[5] The other major problem was the political situation in Andalusia, which Isabel pacified in the course of her long residence in the south from summer 1477 to winter 1478.[6]

3. Orestes Ferrara, *Un pleito sucesorio: Enrique IV, Isabel de Castilla y La Beltraneja* (Madrid, 1945), p. 340.

4. *Crónica incompleta*, pp. 152–53; Suárez, "Guerra de sucesión," pp. 173–75; Fernando del Pulgar, *Crónica de los Reyes Católicos*, 2 vols., ed. Juan de Mata Carriazo, Colección de crónicas españoles, nos. 5–6 (Madrid, 1943), 1:79–80; Juan Torres Fontes, "La conquista del marquesado de Villena en el reinado de los Reyes Católicos," *Hispania* 13 (1953):37–151.

5. María Isabel del Val Valdivieso, "Resistencia al dominio señorial durante los últimos años del reinado de Enrique IV," *Hispania* 34 (1974):53–104.

6. Luis Suárez Fernández, *Nobleza y monarquía: Puntos de vista sobre la historia castellana del siglo XV*, 2nd. ed. (Valladolid, 1975), pp. 263, 269; Miguel Angel Ladero Quesada, *Andalucía en el siglo XV: Estudios de historia política* (Madrid, 1973), p. 98.

Also, the long list of grants made by Enrique required the attention of the new rulers. We have seen that Enrique's gifts were harmful for the crown's income, but because many of the grants had been made to individuals who were now staunch Isabelistas, no wholesale revocations were possible. Not surprisingly then, Fernando and Isabel confirmed far more grants than they revoked. Although the Cortes of 1476 and 1480 pled to have the numbers reduced, their requests were not met. In return for fealty, many nobles had their grants confirmed on favorable terms. Those who had been made *hidalgos* kept their new status. And the famous reform of *mercedes* around 1480 did little more than confirm the noble holdings, while actually increasing their percentage share of the total number of *mercedes.*[7]

While the internal pacification was under way, some five years of fighting were necessary to secure peace abroad and undisputed dominion in Castile. Disposing of their Castilian problems would not have been so difficult if Fernando and Isabel had not had to deal with a new factor in Castilian affairs. The novelty was Afonso V of Portugal. Afonso the African was the name he had gained from Portugal's successful seizures of territory on the African coast. Undeterred by suggestions that Fernando and Isabel might treat diplomatically with him, in January 1475 he announced that he would come to Castile at the head of an army and make Juana his wife.

In May 1475 Afonso crossed the Castilian border leading 20,000 men and made for Plasencia, where he intended to link up with the forces of Juana and Pacheco. Their co-ordination was slow, thus allowing their opponents to muster their forces. On 25 May Juana and Afonso were formally betrothed (the marriage was never completed), and they proclaimed themselves king and queen of Castile. On 30 May Juana's manifesto was published. Among clauses listing her claims to the throne and denying

7. Representative confirmations made between 1475 and 1481 to numerous families: Fernández de Córdoba, Osorio, Manrique, Haro, Niño, Castilla, Mendoza, Téllez Girón, Ponce de León, Pimentel; RAH, *Salazar, leg.* K-39, fols. 55–62; *leg.* M-5, fol. 7v; *leg.* M-31, fols. 69v–71; *leg.* M-49, fols. 66–72; *leg.* M-53, fol. 182; *leg.* M-96, *hojas* 289–99v; *leg.* M-117, *hojas* 90–105; *leg.* 0–1, *hojas* 274–79; *leg.* 0–15, *hojas* 281–87; AHN, *Osuna, caja* 1, no. 14; *leg.* 1618, fol. 3; *leg.* 3921, fol. 9. Enrique Cadenas y Vicent, "El valor de los mercedes enriqueñas de hidalguía," *Hidalguía* 14 (1966):291–94. For the *mercedes* "reform" see Stephen Haliczer, "The Castilian Aristocracy and the Mercedes Reform of 1478-1482," *Hispanic American Historical Review* 55 (1975):449–67.

Isabel any right to be considered queen was a statement charging Fernando and Isabel with having poisoned Enrique IV.[8]

The royal couple moved quickly to mount a defense, dividing the realm between them and scouring it for soldiers and captains. Isabel covered Old and New Castile, suffering a miscarriage from the hard riding, while Fernando went north and west. Within two months they had an army of 40,000 at Valladolid. Fernando maneuvered to join battle. In mid-July 1475 the Castilian army moved slowly from Valladolid to Tordesillas. Meanwhile the great nobles with their personal armies arrived to swell the ranks. The plan to use Zamora as a base of operations shattered when Afonso gained control of it. The attacking army found Afonso supreme and by 23 July the Portuguese king was victorious in the field. Fernando and Isabel had lost the first round, but the defeat taught them an important lesson: the battle failed because the military command was fragmented. Success demanded that the command be unified.

The royal couple proved adept at learning the lesson. By the end of the year they had revitalized the army, making it smaller (15,000) but much more effective and better led. In the spring of 1476 Fernando was ready to take the field again. This time at Toro he defeated the army of Afonso. Perhaps the victory was not as great as it has sometimes been portrayed, but Fernando and Isabel brilliantly exploited their success. Ceremonies of thanksgiving were staged all over Castile. Afonso crossed back into his own country with his army and his intended bride, whose marriage plans were in abeyance.

The major threat to Fernando and Isabel disappeared with the last of the Portuguese troops. In the next months most of the remaining *grandes* made their peace with the royal couple. Afonso V still opposed them for several years. He tried to enlist the aid of Louis XI, but the French monarch knew by then that he would have little success in the peninsula. Afonso mounted an invasion force in early 1479, but one defeat at Albuera on 28 February convinced him to give it up. He entered into peace negotiations and in September the two sides agreed to relinquish the lands each had taken from the other, adjust their differences in the African expansion, exchange prisoners, and reaffirm peace. Isabel's daughter was engaged to Afonso V's grandson. There were involved discussions over Juana's fate,

8. Azcona, *Isabel*, pp. 233–34; Suárez, "Guerra de sucesión," pp. 125–26. Juana the queen outlived her husband by six months. She died on 13 June 1475. The Isabelline chroniclers accuse Afonso of Portugal of having poisoned her, since she was by then an embarrassment. *Crónica incompleta*, p. 196.

and it was suggested that she marry the Castilian prince Juan when he came of age in thirteen years. In the end she decided to enter a convent and took up residence at Santa Clara de Coimbra. She only remained cloistered until 1482 and lived out a long life as the guest of the Portuguese. She never married, and to the end she signed her letters "Yo, la reina."[9]

Even though Enrique IV was not able to leave the crown of Castile to his daughter, he was able to leave a sizable legacy to his kingdom. Enrique was a king who deserved better treatment from posterity than he has received. If the biological and perhaps the legal legacy of Enrique IV was blocked, in a more fundamental sense and more importantly in the long run, Fernando and Isabel maintained, ratified, and completed much of Enrique's legacy as a statesman. He has been denigrated by five centuries of commentators, but Enrique left a set of policies and programs that his successors took over and preserved. Fernando and Isabel were merely successful in implementing them. In the basic trends of Castilian development, the fifteenth century was a period of continuity. The performers changed, but the program remained surprisingly intact.

In his relations with the other kingdoms of western Europe, Enrique's foreign policy was an anticipation of that of his successors. Enrique believed that for Castile, Portugal was more important than the crown of Aragon—an idea that dominated his diplomacy and which may have been more farsighted than is generally acknowledged. The reversal of this policy—the joining of the crowns of Castile and Aragon through marriage—was the result of temporary political contingencies. It was not the culmination of a long historical process, even though such respected historians as Ramón Menéndez Pidal have described the action of Fernando and Isabel as the penultimate movement of the *Reconquista*, an orderly return to the united Spanish monarchy of the Visigoths after seven centuries of division.[10] But it can be forcefully argued that the union of the two crowns was a political marriage of inconvenience, with two kingdoms, dissimilar socially and politically, bound dynastically but never truly united. Tensions between Castile and the eastern periphery have persisted into the twentieth century.

Once the union of Castile and Aragon was a firm reality, Fernando and Isabel then turned wholeheartedly to Enrique's policy of *approchement* to Portugal. After 1479, when the war with Afonso ended, Castile returned to friendship with Portugal and established matrimonial alliances

9. Azcona, *Isabel*, pp. 295–96.

10. Ramón Menéndez Pidal, "Introducción," vol. 17, part 1, of *Historia de España*, ed. Ramón Menéndez Pidal (Madrid, 1969), pp. xi-cxvi.

between the two royal houses. The long-range outcome was Philip II's absorption of Portugal in 1580. Thereafter, Portuguese sentiment came to oppose the union and after sixty years the two countries again separated. If they had been peacefully unified through marriage in the fifteenth century, with all parties agreeing that the heir would inherit both crowns, union might have been more feasible and the Atlantic interests of both countries might have been a cause of unity, not rivalry.

To the north we have seen how relations with France faltered and Castile moved toward association with England and closer ties with the Low Countries. The *Reyes Católicos* sealed these patterns with royal marriages, done mainly to protect Aragon and Aragon's Italian designs by building a diplomatic wall around France. The outcome was the Habsburg inheritance, which through dynastic chance gave Charles V authority over vast territories. This was an unforseen, but no illogical, consequence of patterns predating the coming of Fernando and Isabel. So even here the royal couple cannot be seen as innovators. Long before their accession, Castilian policy was committed to trade with Flanders and was becoming friendlier to England. This was partly the result of royal displeasure after Enrique's meeting with Louis XI, but it was also supported by trading interests in the northern cities of Castile. When Castile joined Aragon in the newly united Spain, Castilian diplomatic orientations reinforced those of Aragon.

Enrique's policy toward Granada—slow pressure and diplomatic thrusts combined with trade and tribute—was altered by the new rulers. Their all-out conquest consumed over a decade and absorbed great resources. While their approach was dissimilar, they did make very effective use of three of the weapons forged by Enrique: the standing royal army, direct crown control of the military orders, and the *Hermandades*.

We have seen that in internal affairs Enrique had very similar appointment practices for royal officials, especially in his use of *letrados*, and he acted to bolster central power by placing royal officials in municipal governments. His policy was not as comprehensive as that of his successors. They were the first to generalize the use of *corregidores* by placing them in all significant Castilian towns, but the beginnings were present in Enrique's reign. Neither Enrique nor his successors allowed the Cortes any latitude; in both reigns it was neglected, relegated to the role of raising subsidies. With the urban brotherhoods, the *Hermandades*, Fernando and Isabel effectively built on Enrique's national reorganization of 1473 and employed the *Hermandades* for the pacification of the kingdom and in the wars against Portugal and Granada.

In royal economic policy Enrique anticipated the reforms of Fernando and Isabel with his *Cuaderno de alcabalas* in 1462, his attempt in 1471 to reform the coinage, and his proposed standardization of weights and measures. But the economic policy of the two reigns is most dramatically distinct in regard to the Mesta and the role of grazing in the Castilian economy. Enrique favored the cloth industry of Castile in his decree that one-third of all raw wool produced in the kingdom should be retained there for domestic use. Fernando and Isabel chose to favor the Mesta, granting it excessive privileges and solidifying the traditional Castilian tendency toward internal production and external commerce of raw materials, mainly wool. Their motivation seems to have been based on a desire to secure the highest return for the crown through proven means and sources of taxation. They did receive the tax revenue desired, but their favor for the grazing interests was at the expense of other sectors of the economy. By so doing they pressed the Castilian economy into a dangerously unitary mold that precluded all but the most minimal development of agriculture and industry in the sixteenth century.[11]

In the problems of Christian orthodoxy and relations with non-Christian groups, we find little divergence between the ideas of Enrique and those of his successors. Enrique exhibited the traditional Castilian royal tolerance toward Muslims and Jews, but he was a committed Christian king and not blind to the increasingly suspect fidelity of some converts from Judaism to Christianity. Here we find another anticipation of his successors' attitudes. When questions arose concerning the sincerity of certain *conversos*, Enrique's response was to create a panel of bishops to investigate. But his action was limited, nothing like the feared and repressive Spanish Inquisition established by Fernando and Isabel, with the forced conversions and expulsions that accompanied it.

Despite the obvious anticipation and strong elements of continuity, the fact remains that Fernando and Isabel did triumph where Enrique had failed. In their long reign they stabilized Castile and laid the foundations for two centuries of Habsburg rule. They brought the nobles into line, but the *grandes* retained their lands and titles and most of their offices, while maintaining a virtual monopoly over the economy. They established a superficial Christian unity, with the loss of economically useful members

11. This is most completely developed in Jaime Vicens Vives, with Jorge Nadal, *An Economic History of Spain*, trans. Frances M. López-Morillas (Princeton, 1969), pp. 291–314. This section has been reprinted in Roger Highfield, ed., *Spain in the Fifteenth Century* (New York and London, 1972), pp. 248–75.

of society and with the imposition of closely monitored intellectual and religious conformity. They established Spain's American empire, but that was an unforeseen happenstance and here too Enrique's disposition of Gibraltar may have served them as a juridical guide for the retention of crown rights in newly conquered lands. They did reorganize the government and establish the conciliar system which was the basis of Habsburg administration. This was new ground; Enrique did nothing in this sphere, although his appointment practices were a useful starting point.

In a larger context we can discern that greater forces were at work and recognize that the failure of Enrique and the qualified success of Fernando and Isabel were due to their different responses to the crisis of fifteenth-century Castile. As we have seen, religious intolerance was on the rise, together with a perilous confrontation between nobles and the crown. In the first matter Enrique moved toward harsher policies regarding non-Christians and maintained slow but steady pressure on the Muslims across the southern frontier. In the second he attempted to dilute the power of the *grandes* by advancing supporters into the higher echelons. In both cases his solutions were ineffectual. In all probability he misjudged the rise of intolerance, and he certainly was not decisive enough in his relations with the nobility. To give Enrique's successors due credit, they were shrewder at judging the tides of their epoch. Although they took some time in doing it, they redirected royal policy to take into consideration the intense hostility of the Old Christian population against Jews, *conversos*, and Muslims. From their restructuring came the Inquisition and the expulsions. In the case of the nobility, the *Reyes Católicos* rendered them less of a political threat by the means we have discussed. In fact, their Granadan policy of total conquest may have been engendered in part by their desire to direct the aggressive instincts of the nobility toward politically acceptable goals. So the failure of the first reign and the success of the second may have been due in no small measure to the fact that Fernando and Isabel had a better appreciation of the complex situation threatening the Castilian crown and found the necessary set of solutions which had eluded Enrique IV. Their responses were firm and comprehensive, where his had been faltering and piecemeal.

But his task was harder than theirs. Enrique IV faced threats on three fronts: Granada, Aragon, and his own nobility in Castile. If at times he appeared inept, faltering, and ineffectual, it is in large part because he could not devote his undivided attention and energies to any one of the three problems. Nevertheless, Enrique made brave efforts to deal with his obstacles. The time has come to recognize and acknowledge that many of the standard assumptions about that unfortunate king are myths. Lamentably, such myths have a vigorous life of their own, and it will be some time before they are finally laid to rest. It is both regrettable and ironic that while Enrique tried to institute sound policies and failed, history recalls the failure and not the attempt. For too long Fernando and Isabel have been praised for their achievements. In numerous ways Enrique's little-appreciated policies were identical to those of the *Reyes Católicos*, in some ways possibly superior. If he cannot be completely rehabilitated, he should at least be accorded an honorable place among the founders of the Spanish monarchy.

ROYAL GRANTS AND APPOINTMENTS

Year	Grants To Individuals		Grants To Corporate Bodies	Appointments Of Officials		Titles Granted
	Enrique IV	Alfonso	Enrique IV	Enrique IV	Alfonso	Enrique IV
1454	12		16	12		0 (26 existing)
1455	11		15	65.7		4
1456	9		10	42.7		0
1457	11		11	51.7		0
1458	4		4	79.7		1
1459	5		6	34.7		2
1460	7		4	47.7		2
1461	6		0	45.7		1
1462	5		4	48.7		2
1463	4		5	33.7		0
1464	16		5	50.7		1
1465	29	39	29	105.7	59	7
1466	18	11	11	71.7	30	1
1467	5	5	4	45.7	16	0
1468	8	9	9	29.7	4	0
1469	29		4	15.7		3
1470	24		4	16.7		3
1471	12		4	15.7		0
1472	17		3	15.7		1
1473	5		2	17.7		1
1474	11		0	15.7		4

Sources:

For grants to individuals and corporate bodies: AGS, *Mercedes y privilegios*; AHN, *Osuna*; RAH, *Salazar*; Torres Fontes, *Itinerario*; and some from narrative sources.

For appointments of officials: AGS, *Quitaciones de Corte* and *Nóminas de Corte*. The figures for Enrique's appointments are calculated by adding (1) the number of appointments identified by year, and (2) the yearly average of appointments not identified by year.

For titles granted: Newton, "Castilian Peerage."

BIBLIOGRAPHY

I. PRIMARY SOURCES

ARCHIVAL COLLECTIONS

Archivo de la Corona de Aragón (Barcelona)
Archivo General de Simancas
Archivo Histórico Nacional (Madrid)
Biblioteca Nacional (Madrid)
Real Academia de la Historia (Madrid)

PRINTED DOCUMENTS (Chronicles and Collections)

Barrientos, Lope. *Refundición de la Crónica del halconero.* Edited by Juan de Mata Carriazo. Colección de crónicas españoles, no. 9. Madrid, 1946.

Basin, Thomas. *Histoire de Louis XI.* Translated and edited by Charles Samaran and Monique-Cécile Garaud. 3 vols. Paris, 1963-72.

Carrillo de Huete, Pedro. *Crónica del halconero de Juan II.* Edited by Juan de Mata Carriazo. Colección de crónicas españoles, no. 8. Madrid, 1946.

Colección de documentos inéditos para la historia de España. Edited by Martín Fernández Navarrete, *et al.* 112 vols. Madrid, 1842-95.

Commynes, Philippe de. *Memoirs: The Reign of Louis XI, 1461-83.* Translated by Michael Jones. Harmondsworth, 1972.

Cortes de los antiguos reinos de León y de Castilla. Edited by the Real Academia de la Historia. 5 vols. Madrid, 1861-1903.

Crónica de Don Alvaro de Luna: Condestable de Castilla, Maestre de Santiago. Edited by Juan de Mata Carriazo. Colección de crónicas españoles, no. 2. Madrid, 1940.

Crónica incompleta de los Reyes Católicos (1469-1476). Edited by Julio Puyol. Madrid, 1934.

Ehingen, Jörg von. *The Diary of Jörg von Ehingen.* Translated and edited by Malcolm Letts. London, 1929.

Enríquez del Castillo, Diego. *Crónica del rey Don Enrique el cuarto de este nombre.* Edited by Cayetano Rosell. *Biblioteca de autores españoles,* vol. 70. Madrid, 1953.

Fernández Alonso, Justo, ed. *Legaciones y nunciaturas en España de 1466 a 1521*. Vol. 1: *1466-1486*. Rome, 1963.

Galíndez de Carvajal, Lorenzo. *Crónica de Enrique IV*. In *Estudio sobre la "Crónica de Enrique IV" del Dr. Galíndez de Carvajal*, by Juan Torres Fontes. Murcia, 1946.

García de Santa María, Alvar. *Crónica de Don Juan II de Castilla, años 1420–1434*. In *Colección de documentos inéditos para la historia de España*, vols. 99–100.

Hechos del Condestable Don Miguel Lucas de Iranzo. Edited by Juan de Mata Carriazo. Colección de crónicas españoles, no. 3. Madrid, 1941.

Machiavelli, Niccòlo. *The Prince*. Translated and edited by T.G. Bergin. New York, 1947.

Maldonaldo, Alonso de. *Hechos del Maestre de Alcántara, Don Alonso de Monrroy*. Edited by Antonio R. Rodríquez Moñino. Madrid, 1935.

Memorias de Don Enrique IV de Castilla. Vol. 2: *Colección diplomática*. Edited by the Real Academia de la Historia. Madrid, 1835-1913.

Millares Carlo, Agustín, ed. *Contribuciones documentales a la historia de Madrid*. Madrid, 1971.

Münzer, J. "Relación del viaje." Translated by Julio Puyol. In *Viajes de extranjeros por España y Portugal*, vol. 1. Edited by J. García Mercadal. Madrid, 1952.

Palencia, Alonso de. *Crónica de Enrique IV*. Translated by Antonio Paz y Meliá. *Biblioteca de autores españoles*, vols. 207–208. Madrid, 1973-75.

Pérez de Guzmán, Fernán. *La crónica del serenísimo príncipe Don Juan, segundo rey deste nombre en Castilla y en León*. Edited by Cayetano Rosell. *Biblioteca de autores españoles*, vol. 68. Madrid, 1953.

——. *Generaciones y semblanzas*. Edited by R.B. Tate. London, 1965.

Pulgar, Fernando del. *Claros varones de Castilla*. Edited by R.B. Tate. Oxford. 1971.

——. *Crónica de los Reyes Católicos*. Edited by Juan de Mata Carriazo. 2 vols. *Colección de crónicas españoles*, nos. 5–6. Madrid, 1943.

Sánchez de Arévalo, Rodrigo. *El vergel de los príncipes*. Edited by Mario Penna. *Biblioteca de autores españoles*, vol. 116. Madrid, 1959.

Sobrequés Callicó, Jaime, ed. *Catálogo de la cancillería de Enrique IV de Castilla, señor del Principado de Cataluña (Lugartenencia de Juan de Beaumont, 1462-1464)*. Barcelona, 1975.

Torre, Antonio de la, and Suárez Fernández, Luis, eds. *Documentos referentes a las relaciones con Portugal durante el reinado de los Reyes Católicos*. Vol. 1. Valladolid, 1958.

The Travels of Leo of Rozmital. Translated and edited by Malcolm Letts. Hakluyt Society Publications, 2nd series, no. 108. Cambridge, 1957.

Valera, Diego de. *Memorial de diversas hazañas*. Edited by Juan de Mata Carriazo. Colección de crónicas españoles, no. 4. Madrid, 1941.

II. SECONDARY SOURCES

Amador de los Ríos, José. *Historia social, política y religiosa de los Judíos de España.* 3 vols. Madrid, 1875.

Amézaga, Elías. *Enrique Cuarto.* Madrid, 1974.

Azcona, Tarsicio de. *Isabel de Castilla: Estudio crítico sobre su vida y su reinado.* Madrid, 1964.

Baer, Yitzhak. *A History of the Jews in Christian Spain.* 2 vols. Philadelphia, 1961-66.

Baron, Salo Wittmayer. *A Social and Religious History of the Jews.* Multivolume. Philadelphia, New York, and London, continuing.

Beinart, Haim. "The Converso Community in 15th Century Castile." *The Sephardi Heritage: Essays in the History and Cultural Contribution of the Jews of Spain and Portugal.* Edited by R.D. Barnett. 2 vols. London, 1971.

Beltrán de Heredía, V. "Las bulas de Nicolás V acerca de los conversos de Castilla." *Sefarad* 21 (1961):22–47.

Benito Ruano, Eloy. "Granada o Constantinopla." *Hispania* 20 (1960): 267–314.

——. *Los infantes de Aragón.* Madrid, 1952.

——. *Toledo en el siglo XV: Vida política.* Madrid, 1961.

Bermejo de la Rica, Antonio. *El triste destino de Enrique IV y La Beltraneja.* Madrid, n. d. [1945].

Bernis, Carmen. "Modas moriscas en la sociedad cristiana española del siglo XV y principios del XVI." *Boletín de la Real Academia de la Historia* 144 (1959):199-228.

Bishko, Charles Julian. "The Peninsular Background of Latin American Cattle Ranching." *Hispanic American Historical Review* 32 (1952): 491–515.

Bonilla y San Martín, Adolfo. *Fernando de Córdoba (1425-1486) y los orígenes del renacimiento filosófico en España.* Madrid, 1911.

Cadenas y Vicent, Enrique. "El valor de los mercedes enriqueñas de hidalguía." *Hidalguía* 14 (1966):291–94.

Canellas López, Angel. "El reino de Aragón en el siglo XV (1410-79)." *Historia de España*, vol. 15. Edited by Ramón Menéndez Pidal. Madrid, 1964.

Cano de Gardoqui, J.L., and Bethencourt, A. de. "Incorporación de Gibraltar a la corona de Castilla (1436-1508)." *Hispania* 26 (1966): 324–81.

Carande, Ramón. *Siete estudios de historia de España.* Barcelona, 1969.

Carlé, María del Carmen. "Mercaderes en Castilla (1252-1512)." *Cuadernos de Historia de España* 21–22 (1954):146–328.

Caro Baroja, Julio. *Los Judíos en la España moderna y contemporánea.* 3 vols. Madrid, 1961.

Carus-Wilson, Eleanora Mary. *Medieval Merchant Venturers*. 2nd ed. London, 1967.

Castro, Américo. *The Spaniards: An Introduction to their History*. Translated by W.F. King and S. Margaretten. Berkeley, Los Angeles, and London, 1971.

Cuartero y Huerta, Baltasar. *El pacto de los Toros de Guisando y la venta del mismo nombre*. Madrid, 1952.

Eisenberg, Daniel. "Enrique IV and Gregorio Marañón." *Renaissance Quarterly* 29 (1976):21–29.

Esteve Barba, Francisco. *Alfonso Carrillo de Acuña: Autor de la unidad de España*. Madrid, 1943.

Fernández-Armesto, Felipe. *Ferdinand and Isabella*. New York, 1975.

Ferrara, Orestes. *Un pleito sucesorio: Enrique IV, Isabel de Castilla y La Beltraneja*. Madrid, 1945.

García de Cortázar, José Angel. *Vizcaya en el siglo XV: Aspectos sociales y económicos*. Bilbao, 1966.

Gimeno Casalduero, Joaquín. *La imagen del monarca en la Castilla del siglo XIV: Pedro el Cruel, Enrique II y Juan I*. Madrid, 1972.

Goñi Gaztambide, José. *Historia de la bula de cruzada en España*. Vitoria, 1958.

Haliczer, Stephen. "The Castilian Aristocracy and the Mercedes Reform of 1478-1482." *Hispanic American Historical Review* 55 (1975):449–67.

Hamilton, Earl J. *American Treasure and the Price Revolution in Spain, 1501-1650*. Cambridge, Mass., 1934; New York, 1965.

Heers, Jacques. *Gênes au XVe siècle: Activité économique et problèmes sociaux*. Paris, 1961.

——. *L'Occident aux XIVe et XVe siècles: Aspects économiques et sociaux*. 2nd ed. Paris, 1966.

Highfield, Roger. "The Catholic Kings and the Titled Nobility of Castile." *Europe in the Late Middle Ages*. Edited by John Hale, J.R.L. Highfield, and Beryl Smalley. London, 1965.

——, ed. *Spain in the Fifteenth Century, 1360-1516: Essays and Extracts by Historians of Spain*. New York and London, 1972.

Huetz de Lemps, Alain. *Vignobles et vins du nord-ouest de l'Espagne*. 2 vols. Bordeaux, 1967.

Kamen, Henry. *The Spanish Inquisition*. New York, 1968.

Klein, Julius. *The Mesta: A Study in Spanish Economic History, 1273-1836*. Cambridge, Mass., 1920.

Konetzke, Richard. "Entrepreneurial Activities of Spanish and Portuguese Noblemen in Medieval Times." *Explorations in Entrepreneurial History* 6 (1953):115–20.

——. *El imperio español: Orígenes y fundamentos*. Translated by Felipe González Vicén. Madrid, 1946.

Ladero Quesada, Miguel Angel. *Andalucía en el siglo XV: Estudios de historia política*. Madrid, 1973.

———. *Castilla y la conquista del reino de Granada.* Valladolid, 1967.

———. *Granada: Historia de un país islámico (1232-1571).* Madrid, 1967.

———. *La hacienda real de Castilla en el siglo XV.* La Laguna, 1973.

Layna Serrano, Francisco. *Historia de Guadalajara y sus Mendozas en los siglos XV y XVI.* 4 vols. Madrid, 1942.

Lea, Henry Charles. *A History of the Inquisition of Spain.* 4 vols. New York, 1906-1907.

Lopez, Robert Sabatino. "El origen de la oveja merina." *Estudios de historia moderna* 4 (1954):1-13.

Lucas-Dubreton, J. *El rey huraño: Enrique IV de Castilla y su época.* Translated by J. García Mercadal. Madrid, 1945.

Lunenfeld, Marvin. *The Council of the Santa Hermandad: A Study of the Pacification Forces of Ferdinand and Isabella.* Coral Gables, Fla., 1970.

MacDonald, I.I. *Don Fernando de Antequera.* Oxford, 1948.

MacKay, Angus. "Popular Movements and Pogroms in Fifteenth-Century Castile." *Past and Present* 55 (1972):33-67.

Marañón, Gregorio. "Ensayo biológico sobre Enrique IV de Castilla." *Boletín de la Real Academia de la Historia* 96 (1930):11-93.

———. *Ensayo biológico sobre Enrique IV de Castilla y su tiempo.* 10th ed. Madrid, 1964.

Mariéjol, Jean Hippolyte. *The Spain of Ferdinand and Isabella.* Translated and edited by Benjamin Keen. New Brunswick, N.J., 1961. First published as *L'Espagne sous Ferdinand et Isabelle.* Paris, 1892.

Márques Villanueva, Francisco. "The Converso Problem: An Assessment." *Collected Studies in Honour of Américo Castro's Eightieth Year.* Edited by M.P. Hornik. Oxford, 1965.

———. "Conversos y cargos concejiles en el siglo XV." *Revista de archivos, bibliotecas y museos* 63 (1957):503-40.

Menéndez Pidal, Ramón. "Introducción." *Historia de España*, vol. 17, part 1. Edited by Ramón Menéndez Pidal. Madrid, 1969.

Merriman, Roger Bigelow. *The Rise of the Spanish Empire in the Old World and the New.* 4 vols. New York, 1918-34.

Miller, Townsend. *Henry IV of Castile, 1425-1474.* Philadelphia and New York, 1972.

Moxó, Salvador de. *La alcabala: Sobre sus orígenes, concepto y naturaleza.* Madrid, 1963.

———. "Los Cuadernos de alcabalas: Orígenes de la legislación tributaria castellana." *Anuario de historia del derecho español* 39 (1969):317-67.

———. "De la nobleza vieja a la nobleza nueva: La transformación nobiliaria castellana en la baja Edad Media." *Cuadernos de historia,* vol. 3. Madrid, 1969.

Newton, Lowell W. "The Development of the Castilian Peerage." Unpublished Ph. D. dissertation. Tulane University, 1972.

O'Callaghan, J.F. "Don Pedro Girón: Master of the Order of Calatrava." *Hispania* 21 (1961):342–90.

Paz y Meliá, Antonio. *El cronista Alonso de Palencia: Su vida y sus obras, sus Décadas y las crónicas contemporáneas*. Madrid, 1904.

Pérez-Embid, Florentino. "Navigation et commerce dans le port de Séville au bas moyen âge." *Moyen Age* 3–4 (1969):263–89, 479–502.

Pescador del Hoyo, María del Carmen. "Los orígenes de la Santa Hermandad." *Cuadernos de historia de España* 55–56 (1972):400–43.

Plaza Bores, Angel de la. *Archivo General de Simancas: Guía del Investigador*. Valladolid, 1962.

Prescott, William H. *History of the Reign of Ferdinand and Isabella*. 3 vols. Philadelphia, 1872.

Puyol Alonso, Julio. "Los cronistas de Enrique IV." *Boletín de la Real Academia de la Historia* 78 (1921):399–415, 448–96; 79 (1921):11–28, 118–41.

Rodríquez Villa, Antonio. *Bosquejo biográfico de Don Beltrán de la Cueva*. Madrid, 1881.

Rumeu de Armas, Antonio. *España en el Africa atlántica*. 2 vols. Madrid, 1956–57.

Sánchez-Albornoz, Claudio. *España: Un enigma histórico*. 2 vols. Buenos Aires, 1962.

Serrano, Luciano. *Los Reyes Católicos y la ciudad de Burgos, desde 1451 a 1492*. Madrid, 1943.

Sitges, Juan Blas. *Enrique IV y la excelente Señora llamada vulgarmente Doña Juana la Beltraneja, 1425-1530*. Madrid, 1912.

Sobrequés Callicó, Jaime. "Enric IV de Castella, seynor del principat de Catalunya." *La Guerra civil catalana del segle XV*, vol. 1. Edited by S. Sobrequés. Barcelona, 1973. Pp. 301–464.

Sobrequés Vidal, Santiago. "La época del patriciado urbano." *Historia social y económica de España y América*, vol. 2. Edited by Jaime Vicens Vives. Barcelona, 1957.

Suárez Fernández, Luis. "La guerra de sucesión." *Historia de España*, vol. 17, part 1. Edited by Ramón Menéndez Pidal. Madrid, 1969.

———. *Juan I, Rey de Castilla (1379-1390)*. Madrid, 1955.

———. *Juan II y la frontera de Granada*. Valladolid, 1954.

———. *Nobelza y monarquía: Puntos de vista sobre la historia castellana del siglo XV*. Valladolid, 1959; 2nd ed. 1975.

———. "En torno al pacto de los Toros de Guisando." *Hispania* 23 (1963): 344–65.

———. "Los Trastámaras de Castilla y Aragón en el siglo XV (1407-74)." *Historia de España*, vol. 15. Edited by Ramón Menéndez Pidal. Madrid, 1964.

———, and Rodríquez Valencia, Vicente. *Matrimonio y derecho sucesorio de Isabel la Católica*. Valladolid, 1960.

Tate, Robert B. *Ensayos sobre la historiografía peninsular del siglo XV*. Translated by Jesus Días. Madrid, 1970.

Torres Fontes, Juan. "La conquista del marquesado de Villena en el reinado de los Reyes Católicos." *Hispania* 13 (1953):37–151.

____. "La contratación de Guisando." *Anuario de estudios medievales* 2 (1965):399–428.

____. *Don Pedro Fajardo, adelantado de Murcia.* Madrid, 1953.

____. *Estudio sobre la "Crónica de Enrique IV" del Dr. Galíndez de Carvajal.* Murcia, 1946.

____. *Fajardo el Bravo.* Murcia, 1944.

____. *Itinerario de Enrique IV de Castilla.* Murcia, 1955.

____. *El príncipe Don Alfonso, 1465-1468.* Murcia, 1971.

____. "Las treguas con Granada de 1462 y 1463." *Hispania* 23 (1963): 163–99.

Trame, Richard H. *Rodrigo Sánchez de Arévalo, 1404-1470: Spanish Diplomat and Champion of the Papacy.* Washington, D.C., 1958.

Val Valdivieso, María Isabel del. *Isabel la Católica, Princesa (1468-1474).* Valladolid, 1974.

____. "Resistencia al dominio señorial durante los últimos años del reinado de Enrique IV." *Hispania* 34 (1974):53–104.

Valdeavellano, Luis G. de. *Curso de historia de las instituciones españoles de los orígenes al final de la Edad Media.* 4th ed. Madrid, 1975.

Valdeón Baruque, Julio. *Enrique II de Castilla: La guerra civil y la consolidación del régimen (1366-1371).* Valladolid, 1966.

____. *Los Judíos de Castilla y la revolución Trastámara.* Valladolid, 1968.

Vicens Vives, Jaime. *Approaches to the History of Spain.* Translated by Joan C. Ullman. Berkeley and Los Angeles, 1967.

____. *Historia crítica de la vida y reinado de Fernando II de Aragón.* Zaragoza, 1962.

____. *Juan II de Aragón (1398-1479): Monarquía y revolución en la España del siglo XV.* Barcelona, 1953.

____. "Los Trastámaras y Cataluña." *Historia de España,* vol. 15. Edited by Ramón Menéndez Pidal. Madrid, 1964.

____. With Jorge Nadal. *An Economic History of Spain.* Translated by Frances M. López-Morillas. Princeton, 1969.

Wolff, Philippe. "The 1391 Pogrom in Spain: Social Crisis or Not?" *Past and Present* 50 (1971):4–18.